The Warrior Mom's Guide to Living in Peace

Peaceful End-of-Life Planning for Moms Living with Chronic Illness

Author Shaundra M. G. Harris

The Warrior Mom's Guide to Living in Peace

Peaceful End-of-Life Planning for Moms Living with Chronic Illness

Author Shaundra M. G. Harris

Shaun The Mom Publishing

© 2025 Shaundra M. G. Harris.

All rights reserved.

Paperback ISBN 978-1-969446-03-0

Hardcover ISBN: 978-1-969446-13-9

First Edition

No part of this publication may be reproduced, stored in a retrieval system, or transmitted in any form without written permission from the author, except by reviewers or educators using brief quotations with proper citation.

Publisher Shaun The Mom Publishing

Printed in the United States.

www.warriormomacademy.com

Disclaimer

This book is intended for informational and inspirational purposes only. The content reflects the personal experiences, opinions, and insights of the author and should not be considered a substitute for professional medical, legal, financial, educational, therapeutic, or spiritual advice.

While the author shares tools, tips, and resources that have been personally helpful, every situation is unique. Readers are encouraged to consult with qualified professionals before making decisions regarding health, finances, homeschooling, parenting, estate planning, or other matters discussed in this book.

Some links or references provided may be affiliate links. This means the author may receive a small commission at no extra cost to you if you choose to purchase through those links. These recommendations are made in good faith and only include resources the author personally uses or believes may be helpful.

Any printable templates, checklists, or workbook materials included are for personal use only and may not be distributed, sold, or used commercially without written permission from the author.

The author and publisher expressly disclaim any liability arising directly or indirectly from the use or misuse of any information, tools, or resources included in this book.

To every mother who has ever laid awake in the dark, wondering how her children would go on without her—

To my children Aoki, Layla, Jayden, Nia.

Welcome

This book is for you.

For the fierce, tender love that makes you plan for things no one wants to think about.

For the strength it takes to face your own fears so your children never have to.

For the hope that, even when you are gone, your love will remain—guiding, protecting, and holding them.

You are not alone.

Your courage is your legacy.

Table of Contents

Introduction 12
- **Dear Mama, Read This First** 12
- **From Survival to Purpose** 17
- **Why We All Need a Plan** 25
- **Love, Not Fear: Why This Book Exists** 35

Part I: Preparing Your Heart and Home ... 36
- **Chapter 1: Facing the Future with Courage** ... 37
- **Chapter 2: Talking to Your Children** 42
- **Chapter 3: Creating Meaningful Memories** ... 46
- **Chapter 4 : Creating a Peaceful Home Environment** 49

Part II: Understanding and Documenting Your Wishes 54
- **Chapter 5: Understanding End-of-Life Documents** 55
- **Chapter 6: What Is Estate Planning?** 58
- **Chapter 7: Which Legal Documents Do I Need?** 61
- **Chapter 8: Organizing and Storing Your Important Documents** 64
- **Chapter 9: Common Estate Planning Mistakes** 69
- **Chapter 10: The Risks of Not Having an Estate Plan** 72

Part III: Guardianship, Care, and Special Considerations 75

Chapter 11: Guardianship and Care Decisions 76

Chapter 12: Planning for Guardianship of Minor Children 79

Chapter 13: Planning for Loved Ones with Special Needs 84

Chapter 14: Choosing a Power of Attorney and Healthcare Proxy 90

Part IV: Financial Planning and Protecting Your Legacy 96

Chapter 15: Building Your Financial Footprint — Protecting Your Children's Future 97

Chapter 16: Inheritance Planning with Intention — Leaving More Than Money 104

Chapter 17: Creating or Updating Your Will 110

Chapter 18: Setting Up a Living Trust 115

Chapter 19: Planning for Your Business and Succession 121

Part V: Digital Assets, Communication, and Maintenance 125

Chapter 20: Managing Digital Assets and Your Online Legacy 126

Chapter 21: Updating and Maintaining Your Estate Plan 132

Chapter 22: Estate Plan Annual Review Checklist 137

Chapter 23: Estate Plan Update Action Plan 141

Chapter 24: Communicating Your Plan with Loved Ones 143

Part VI: Community, Grief, and Healing. 148

Chapter 25: Community, Support, and Spiritual Strength 149

Chapter 26: Memory, Celebration, and Ritual 155

Chapter 27: Losing a Parent or Loved One .. 159
Checklist: After a Loved One Passes 166

Part VII: Your Legacy of Love 169

Chapter 28: Set Your Estate Planning Goals 170

Chapter 29: Your Legacy of Love................. 180

A Letter to My Readers 182

Scriptures for Peace & Eternal Hope 184

Book Club / Group Discussion Questions 185

Glossary of Key Terms 186

Resources and Support 192

The Warrior Mom's Guide™ Book Series 194

About the Author...................................... 198

Acknowledgments 199

Introduction

Dear Mama, Read This First

This guide was created for moms like us—the ones who love hard, worry harder, and sometimes carry the weight of the world on our shoulders, especially when it comes to our babies.

I didn't start this journey just because I was afraid of dying. I started it because I was tired of being too anxious to really live. I spent too many days stuck in fear, unable to enjoy the beauty right in front of me. Always wondering: What would happen to my children if I wasn't here tomorrow?

Then something shifted.

If the fear was going to live in my mind anyway, I decided to give it a job. Instead of letting it paralyze me, I let it push me. I faced the hard questions. I made a plan. And let me tell you—the freedom that came from that? Life-changing.

It didn't just give my kids a safer future. It gave me back my present.

As a mom living with sickle cell, I know there will be hard days—days when I need rest, days when the pain takes over. But on the good days? I want to be free. Free to laugh with my children. Free to garden. Free to dance in my kitchen (yes—even while cooking, something I used to dread). And now, I am free. Because I've handled the heavy stuff.

That's what I want for you, too.

This guide isn't about fear. It's about peace. It's about preparing not just your children for the day you may no longer be here, but preparing yourself to live more fully now.

Because here's what I've learned:

Life always comes with stress. We're here on Earth—there's baggage. But when you take care of the big stuff in advance, the little stuff doesn't hit as hard. If you've already handled life insurance, a will, maybe even a trust... a flat tire? That's just a lunch break and a call to roadside assistance. You're unbothered. Because you've handled the heavy.

Wealthy people aren't carefree because they have money. They're carefree because they used their money to solve problems. They put systems in place. They don't wait until it's too late. They plan. They set up insurance, trusts, investments—for their kids and their grandkids. It's not luck. It's intention.

But you don't have to be rich to plan like the wealthy.

When you line up your ducks, you don't have to keep looking back to make sure they're still there. You told your money where to go. You told your kids' future what to do. You even told your spirit where you're headed. And that, mama, is power.

If you've been with me since Warrior Within: A Mom's Guide to Thriving with Sickle Cell Anemia and Chronic Illness, maybe you're a little tired from all the work you've already done. I get it. Chronic illness touches every part of our lives—family functions, family finances, everything in between. But we've learned how to care for ourselves and our homes. We've found ways to connect with our loved ones in ways that honor our needs, protect our peace, and uphold our boundaries.

Most importantly, we've been learning to trust God more. The way He shows up for each of us may look different, but if you pause to count your blessings, you'll see they're there.

Now, I'm not saying life is perfect. But I can say that even if I'm not where I want to be, I'm so glad I'm not where I used to be.

Forward is forward.

So let's look forward.

What could your future look like? What might it look like for your kids? If we keep stacking the right habits and routines, eventually our days start to feel more manageable. With patience, diligence, and consistent effort—even with chronic illness—we begin to see the payoff. Financially. Emotionally. Spiritually.

One step at a time, we move out of survival mode and into stability.

This season—the season of stability—might feel strange at first. You'll find yourself looking at your budget thinking, Wait... did I miss a bill? There's money left? Bills will get paid on time. No stress. No scrambling. Just done. That flutter in your chest? That's your new reality settling in.

Embrace it. Let it remind you that things are shifting—and they're shifting for your good.

And as we continue managing the day-to-day, it's time to plan for the future.

Because here's the truth: You might wonder, Why invest or plan if I'm just going to die? Two words: inheritance and compound-interest. (Yes, I made that one word—it's magic.)

The Bible talks about inheritance:

Proverbs 13:22 (NIV):

A good man leaves an inheritance to his children's children, but the sinner's wealth is laid up for the righteous.

This verse highlights the importance of planning for future generations—financially, spiritually, and morally.

And here's another one that my second-ex-not-husband thought was so good he tattooed it on his arm:

1 Timothy 5:8 (ESV):

But if anyone does not provide for his relatives, and especially for members of his household, he has denied the faith and is worse than an unbeliever.

As a single mom, I had to step into that role. A father is supposed to leave homes and wealth to his children. So guess what? I'm going to do it myself.

Just like we're planning for life, we're going to plan for when we're not here anymore.

So let's get this stuff out of the way. Let's handle it.

And then—let's go enjoy our day.

This guide is here to help you free your mind and spirit so you can savor all the days you have left.

With love, purpose, and peace,

Shaun

From Survival to Purpose

I wasn't prepared.

Not for the pain.

Not for the fear.

And certainly not for the possibility that my children might have to live without me.

That's the kind of fear that shakes you to your core—not just the fear of dying, but the fear of leaving this world without a plan. Without knowing who would step in. Who would love, nurture, and protect my babies if I couldn't. That thought haunted me.

Lying in that hospital bed alone, I realized the terrifying truth: I had no one ready to take my place. And I felt like I was running out of time.

Over the past decade, I had been building a life for my family with my fiancé. I was working hard, going to school, doing what I thought would secure our future. But I had missed two essential things: caring for my health—and surrendering my life to God.

I was living out of alignment. Out of wedlock. Allowing dysfunction and distraction into our lives. Slowly, everything began to fall apart: my health, my finances, my parenting, my peace.

Then life hit me hard.

My body gave out. I found myself broke—emotionally, financially, spiritually. I had been trying to build a life in my own strength, ignoring the signs, pushing past the warnings, chasing security through the wrong things.

It all started in a dark room.

I have Sickle Cell Anemia. And I pushed myself far beyond what my body could handle. I kept working through the pain, thinking rest was a luxury I couldn't afford. One day, I collapsed on the curb outside my job—too weak to stand, still trying to clock in.

My supervisor called the ambulance.

Even then, I just wanted to go home and sleep it off. My ex—usually unconcerned—was angry that I had pushed myself that far. But what else was I supposed to do? He was financially irresponsible, and I had been taught to fend for myself. So I worked. Until I couldn't.

In the ER, I needed an immediate blood transfusion. I was completely drained—literally. My body was shutting down: chest pains, exhaustion, pneumonia, acute chest syndrome. My sickle cell was screaming for attention I had denied it for too long.

At that point, I wasn't just sick. I was broken.

Still, I was working midnight shifts, going to school full-time, homeschooling and raising four children—alone. My boyfriend was busy with his own life, and I was drowning under infidelity, poor decisions, stress, and silence.

Even after losing my sister to the same disease, I still hadn't slowed down. No doctors. No medication. No plan. I thought I could out-hustle pain. I thought I could outwork what only healing and faith could fix. But I was wrong.

So God stepped in.

That hospital stay lasted almost three weeks. Alone. Hooked up to machines and IVs. Still answering calls from my children, still ordering food deliveries from my hospital bed. Still trying to parent from what felt like a deathbed.

And then came the moment that changed me forever:

"If I die, who will do this? Who will fight for them like I do? Who will love them like I love them?"

That question shattered me in a way nothing ever had.

I prayed harder than I ever had before. I begged God to let me live. To let me come home. I made a promise:

"God, if You get me home, I will do what needs to be done."

And I already knew what that was.

Deep down, I'd known for years. I had stayed in something toxic too long. I had gone back on a promise I made to God after my first relationship ended at 22—when I'd already been with someone since I was 15. I told God I would take time to grow. I didn't. Instead, I entered another long, unhealthy relationship that pulled me even further from Him.

You can't build a God-honoring life in sin.

You can't be faithful to someone who worships the flesh and expect peace.

You can't build a future with someone who can't manage today.

I had been trying to fix what God had long called me to release. Trying to parent with someone who didn't want to parent. Trying to be led by someone lost.

So, from that hospital bed, I made a new commitment:

I would put God first. I would take care of myself. I would build a future based on faith, not fear.

All the things I was chasing—cars, houses, appearances, security—God had already promised me those. I was working too hard for what He was willing to give freely, if I would just surrender.

And surrender I did.

God didn't gently guide me out. He tore it all down. Pulled me out by the roots and placed my feet on solid ground. Then He said, "Walk."

And I did. Still do.

That's faith—walking through a desert in the dark, trusting the light will come.

When I got out of the hospital, I kept my promise. I left the unhealthy relationship. I started healing—for real this time. I reconnected with God. I poured into my kids. I stopped hustling for survival and started planning for legacy.

I went from food pantries to fully stocked fridges.

From survival mode to strategy.

From chaos to clarity.

And yes—I started preparing for my death. Not out of fear. But out of love.

Because real love doesn't end when we die.

It continues in the plans we leave, the peace we pass down, the clarity we give our children.

That's what this book is about.

It's not sad. It's not morbid. It's freeing. It's a love letter to your people. It's peace on paper. A blueprint. A final gift.

This is my story. From broken to whole. From forgotten to faithful. From fear to fierce belief.

This is your invitation to do the same.

You are a Warrior Mom.

Welcome to the ThriveHive.

Reflection | Prayer | Affirmation | Action
From Survival to Purpose

Reflection Questions
Take a quiet moment. Breathe. Let your heart speak.

1. What fear have you been carrying that you haven't faced yet?
2. Where in your life have you been trying to hustle instead of heal?
3. Are there relationships or patterns that have pulled you away from your faith or your peace?
4. What would it look like to surrender control and trust God with the parts of your life you've been trying to manage alone?
5. If you were to leave this earth tomorrow, what unfinished business would weigh most heavily on your spirit?

Affirmation
I am no longer bound by fear.

I am free to heal, free to trust, and free to prepare a legacy of love.

God is with me in every step—from survival to purpose.

Prayer

Dear God,

I come to You with an open heart. I lay down every fear, every burden, every place where I've tried to do life in my own strength.

Thank You for never leaving me, even when I was far from You. Thank You for the grace that saved me from my own ways.

Help me to trust You fully. Help me to honor this life You've given me by caring for myself, caring for my children, and preparing wisely for whatever lies ahead.

Lead me out of survival and into purpose. Use my story for Your glory.

Amen.

Action Steps

Start right where you are. Small steps matter.

Make a List.

- Write down everything you feel you're carrying alone—responsibilities, fears, old pain, unfinished plans. Seeing it on paper makes it easier to release and prioritize.

Choose One Area to Surrender.

- Ask yourself honestly: Where have I been trying to do this without God? Decide to let Him in today. Pray over that area specifically.

Identify One Next Step Toward Peace.

- Maybe it's calling a doctor. Setting a boundary. Organizing your important documents. Ending an unhealthy relationship. Just pick one step and take it this week.

Speak Your Affirmation Daily.

Write your affirmation somewhere you can see it. Repeat it every morning:

- I am free to heal. I am free to trust. I am preparing a legacy of love.

Why We All Need a Plan

Why you should share this book. This applies to everyone you, your sister, your cousin and friends your momma too. Everyone should be minding their own business and taking care of their own business.

When my sister got sick, it came down to me and my mom to make the decisions. But of course, my mother was too emotional—and rightfully so. I, on the other hand, tend to go straight to the hard questions. That's just how my mind works. It makes me a great planner. Sometimes a worrier, yes—but definitely a planner.

In my family, I'm the anchor. And when the storm hits, what do anchors do? They hold things down. They drag everyone to a safe stop.

My sister was technically an adult, but at the time she was completely incapacitated—medically sedated, in a coma, unable to speak or advocate for herself. That left my mother as the default decision-maker. But she couldn't handle it alone.

She called me—her daughter, and my sister's sister—for support. Thankfully, I was more than just close family. I shared the same illness. I understood the stakes. And I had the ability to think clearly in a crisis.

The Day at the Hospital

Picture this: You're at work and you get a call—come to the hospital, now. Your sister, who had already been a patient for several days, has taken a turn for the worse.

You rush over. The nurse walks you through sterile hallways and leads you into a large, cold conference room.

Your mom is already there, slumped in the corner, her coat pulled over her face, sobbing. You ask what's wrong—no answer. You ask again, voice trembling. Still nothing. Just silence and tears.

Then there's a knock.

The door opens. In walks a doctor. Then another. And another. Before long, the entire room is filled—seats taken, people lining the walls, even voices piped in on conference phones from other hospitals.

I froze. I looked at my mother and whispered, "Is she dead?"

One of the doctors gently replied, "No. But she's very critical."

They began listing complications. Words blurred. I was in shock. My mom, devastated and overwhelmed, had told them she couldn't make the decisions. So they turned to me.

Now it was me. They needed me to decide.

My sister had sickle cell disease. The year before, her lungs collapsed and she had to be airlifted to the University of Michigan. This time, it was worse—and she was pregnant.

Both she and the baby were dying. Her body was attacking itself. The baby's presence made everything worse. Their chances of survival were low. I was asked: Who should we save?

I could have crumbled. But something took over. Call it God, call it instinct, call it grace—I stood up, and I led.

I listened. I made the calls. I told them:

"We're saving them both."

Even though she was sedated and ventilated, I directed the team to prep for an emergency C-section. But not until the University of Michigan confirmed her transfer and the helicopter was ready to fly. I told them to send the baby straight to the NICU. I made sure her care didn't get deprioritized because of the baby. I fought for both of them.

And by the grace of God, the baby—born at 23 weeks, weighing just 1 pound, 3 ounces—survived. He spent nearly five months in the NICU, fighting for every breath.

During surgery, doctors discovered the root of her infection: a septic uterus. The same infection likely responsible for her near-death the year before. Another decision had to be made. Remove her uterus, or risk losing her.

I made the call. Again.

She was transferred to the hospital that had saved her once before. And by another miracle, they saved her again. She lived almost two more years. Her son—our son—is still thriving today.

Why Planning Matters

Here's the truth: I wasn't prepared for any of it. But the decisions still had to be made.

That's why planning is so important. Having someone who knows your wishes—truly knows you—can make the difference between life and death. Because my sister and I were close, I knew what she would want. I knew she'd want me to fight for both her and the baby.

But imagine if I hadn't. Imagine if we hadn't had those talks. If I had made the wrong choice, it could've destroyed our relationship forever. Some decisions you can't undo.

One day, we were joking about the pronunciation of "jalapeños." The next, I was explaining to her everything she'd just been through—waking up in a different hospital, in a different city, no longer able to have children, her baby fighting for his life in the NICU. All of it.

She was in shock. But the emotion she showed most?

Gratitude.

She just kept repeating, "I'm so glad you came."

I told her, "I was just trying to save you and the baby."

She nodded through tears, "I know."

It broke me. I hadn't had time to feel anything. But in that moment, the tears finally came. We didn't speak. We just felt.

Aftermath & The Hard Truths

If we had had a plan—a clear one—things would've been so much easier. A living will. A power of attorney. Medical directives. Anything.

But we didn't.

And after that moment? We never got another chance. She passed away far too young. We didn't have a will. No life insurance. No guardianship instructions. No banking or financial details. We had to dig through papers and piece everything together during the worst grief of our lives.

Everyone had opinions. Everyone thought they knew what she wanted. But we had no official guidance—just heartbreak and guesswork.

So I'm begging you: don't do that to your loved ones.

Here's What We Needed (And What You Might Need Too):

- A Will
- A Medical Power of Attorney
- A Living Will or Advance Directive
- Life Insurance
- A Financial Plan for her children (trust funds, guardianship arrangements, etc.)

Planning isn't about being morbid. It's about being kind. It's about easing the burden on the people who love you most—so they can focus on healing and celebrating your life, not fighting over your death.

🦋 Reflection | Prayer | Affirmation | Action

Why We All Need a Plan

Reflection

Reading this might have stirred up something in you. Maybe fear. Maybe love. Maybe guilt for not having had these conversations yet.

That's okay.

I didn't have a plan when my sister got sick, either. I didn't know what decisions I would be asked to make, or that I'd be the one standing in a hospital room with life hanging in the balance.

But what I did have was a deep understanding of who my sister was—what she valued, how she fought, and how she loved her children.

That gave me the strength to speak up for her when she couldn't speak for herself.

I want you to imagine someone you love—someone close to you—lying in a hospital bed, unable to communicate. What would they want? Would you know? Would you feel confident making decisions on their behalf?

And now flip it.

What if you were the one in the bed?

Would the people around you know what matters most to you? Would they know who should make those decisions? Would they have the legal authority to do it?

Planning is not about expecting the worst. It's about protecting the people you love when the unexpected happens. Because life is uncertain—but love should never leave people guessing.

Action Steps

Here are some simple but powerful steps you can take today to begin building a plan that protects you and your family:

1. Start the Conversation
   - Talk to your loved ones about your values, your medical preferences, and who you'd trust to make decisions if you couldn't.
   - Ask them the same questions.

2. Designate a Medical Power of Attorney
   - Choose someone you trust to make healthcare decisions on your behalf.
   - Put it in writing. Make it legal.

3. Create a Living Will / Advance Directive
   - Document your wishes regarding life support, resuscitation, and organ donation.
   - Keep it accessible and share it with your family and doctor.

4. Write a Will
   - Decide how you want your assets and responsibilities handled.
   - Appoint a guardian if you have children.

5. Secure Life Insurance and Financial Plans
   - If you have dependents, ensure they're financially protected.
   - Consider a trust or savings plan for your children.

6. Organize Your Information
   - Store important documents in one place (passwords, bank accounts, insurance info, medical history).
   - Let your loved ones know where to find it.

7. Review and Update Regularly
   - Revisit your plan annually or when major life events happen (birth, death, divorce, diagnosis).

Planning isn't about control—it's about love.

It's about giving your family peace of mind in moments of chaos, and clarity when everything else feels uncertain.

You don't need to have everything figured out today. Just take one step. Then another. And another. You'll be surprised how much calmer you'll feel just knowing the groundwork is in place.

Your future self—and your family—will thank you.

Love, Not Fear: Why This Book Exists

There's a kind of strength that no one talks about—the strength it takes to love your children deeply while carrying the weight of uncertainty. If you're reading this, you may be facing a chronic illness, or navigating the reality that your time here may be more limited than you ever imagined.

This book is not about death. It's about love.

It's about preparing with peace in your heart instead of fear. It's about clarity, not confusion. It's about leaving a legacy that says to your children: I thought of you. I protected you. I loved you with everything I had—even in the hardest moments.

As mothers, especially single mothers, we often carry everything on our own. The planning, the emotions, the finances, the futures—it all lives on our shoulders. This guide is here to help you gently unpack that weight and begin making decisions that feel like acts of care, not burdens.

This is your space. To cry. To prepare. To plan with love. To live while you still can.

This is not the end of your story—it's part of the love story you're writing for your children.

Let's begin.

Part I: Preparing Your Heart and Home

Chapter 1: Facing the Future with Courage

"Courage doesn't always roar. Sometimes courage is the quiet voice at the end of the day saying, 'I will try again tomorrow.'" – Mary Anne Radmacher

There's a unique strength that comes from living every day with a chronic illness like sickle cell. You've faced hospitals, pain, and fear—and still found ways to raise your children, build a life, and hold onto hope.

That strength doesn't disappear when you start thinking about what happens after. It becomes a source of wisdom.

Facing mortality isn't giving up—it's loving fiercely.

This chapter is about shifting your mindset. Preparing for the end of life is not surrender; it's an act of deep love. As moms, our instinct is to protect, to plan, to leave something better for our children. That doesn't stop because of a diagnosis. If anything, it becomes even more important.

There's no easy way to think about your own mortality, especially when you're still actively parenting, working, and surviving day to day. But acknowledging the future is not a betrayal of hope—it's a profound act of courage.

In this chapter, we'll talk about what it means to face the unknown, how to process fear without letting it take over, and why preparing now—while you have strength—is a priceless gift to your children.

Mindset shifts

1. Redefining Courage

Courage isn't just fighting to live—it's living well, even when life is uncertain. It's looking fear in the face and still choosing to love, to plan, to show up. Courage can be quiet and still. It can be organizing your documents, writing letters, or having honest conversations about your hopes.

2. Acknowledging the Fear Without Letting It Win

You don't have to be fearless to be brave. Fear is part of this journey. But naming it, writing about it, speaking it aloud—that's how you loosen its grip. Journaling, prayer, therapy, or talking with trusted friends can help you process these feelings safely.

3. Why Now Matters

There's no perfect time to talk about death. But there is power in choosing to do it now, while your voice is strong. You are the expert on your life, your wishes, your values. Preparing now ensures your love and intentions will live on clearly—without confusion or guesswork.

Choosing peace over panic is not expecting to die tomorrow. It's giving your family the comfort of clarity.

4. Legacy Begins Today

Your legacy is already unfolding in the way you show up every day. But legacy can also be intentional. In the next chapters, we'll walk through practical steps to prepare documents, letters, and traditions that will keep your spirit alive. It starts here—with the courage to begin.

🦋 Reflection | Prayer | Affirmation | Action

Facing the Future with Courage

Reflection Questions

1. What does courage look like in your life right now?
2. What fears are you carrying about the future?
3. How can you show love to yourself as you begin this planning process?

Affirmation

I am courageous. I choose love over fear, preparation over avoidance, and peace over panic. My strength is greater than my worry.

Prayer

God, grant me the courage to face the unknown with an open heart.

Help me trust that preparing now is an act of love, not surrender.

Fill me with peace as I take each step to protect the ones I love. Amen.

Action Steps

- Write down one fear you have about preparing—and one way you will face it this week.
- Choose a trusted person you can talk to about your wishes.
- Schedule time this month to begin gathering important documents.

Chapter 2: Talking to Your Children

"Children may not understand everything, but they feel everything."

There are few things harder than looking into your child's eyes and explaining something even adults struggle to understand.

When you live with a chronic illness, you become an expert at protecting your children from your pain.

But as you begin preparing for the future, it's time to gently bring them into the conversation—not to scare them, but to anchor them in love and honesty.

Silence, though well-meaning, leaves space for fear to grow wild. Children are intuitive; they pick up on every shift in energy. Giving them honest, age-appropriate information builds trust and helps them feel secure even when life feels uncertain.

In this chapter, you'll find ways to open the conversation, leave emotional keepsakes, and help your children process feelings and build resilience.

Tips to help you talk to your children

1. Start Where They Are

Every child is different. Consider:

- Toddlers & Preschoolers may not grasp finality but notice changes in routines and moods.
- Elementary-age kids may ask blunt questions and need reassurance they'll be cared for.
- Teens often understand more than they say. They may react with anger or withdrawal before opening up.

It's okay to say, "I don't know," or "This is hard to talk about, but I love you, and I'll always love you."

2. Let the Love Lead

These conversations are about love, not just facts. Reassure them:

- It's okay to feel sad, confused, or scared.
- They are not responsible for your illness.
- You have a plan to keep them safe and surrounded by love.

Remind them your love doesn't end—even when life does.

3. Create Emotional Keepsakes

Begin creating keepsakes that can be returned to when your voice isn't there:

- Letters for birthdays and milestones
- Audio or video messages
- Journals with your hopes for them
- Favorite recipes or songs

These gifts won't replace you—but they will remind your children you were here, and you loved them deeply.

4. Build Emotional Resilience

Grief is a process, and children will walk through it in their own time. You can help by:

- Encouraging creative expression
- Connecting them to a counselor or support group
- Teaching them words for their feelings
- Modeling your own emotional honesty

You don't have to be perfect—just present.

Reflection | Prayer | Affirmation | Action

Talking to Your Children

Reflection Questions

1. What do you most want your child to remember about you?
2. What fears do you have about talking with them?
3. What comforts can you offer them right now?

Affirmation

I am a safe place for my child's feelings. My honesty and love will guide them through every season.

Prayer

God, give me the words to speak with gentleness and truth. Help me reassure my children of my love and Your love that never ends. Surround us with comfort and courage as we share these tender conversations. Amen.

Action Steps

- Schedule a quiet time to begin the conversation with your child.
- Write or record one message to give them later.
- Identify one tradition or keepsake you'd like to start creating together.

Chapter 3: Creating Meaningful Memories

"Legacy isn't just what you leave—it's what you live."

When you're preparing your children for a future without you, it's easy to get caught up in logistics: wills, care plans, documents. Those things matter. But equally important—maybe more so—are the memories you create with the time you have.

This chapter is not about grand gestures. It's about intentional moments. Living with the knowledge that your voice, your presence, your love can linger in the details of their lives.

1. Leave More Than Words—Leave Your Voice

Write letters, but also record videos or audio. Your children will want to hear your laugh and encouragement. Just be you. Talk about what you love about them. Sing. Tell them stories. These will be treasures when they need you most.

2. Create Traditions That Can Outlive You

Start a tradition—Sunday pancakes, bedtime stories, birthday letters. Share why these rituals matter and encourage loved ones to continue them. They will become anchors of love.

3. Capture the Everyday

Take candid pictures. Let your kids take photos of you. Don't worry about looking tired or different. You are still you, and they will treasure every frame.

4. Write the Unspoken

Write letters for future milestones—graduation, marriage, first heartbreak. Create a memory box or time capsule with little reminders of your love.

5. Celebrate the Present Moment

You are still here. Laugh today. Be silly. Be present. Even on hard days, memories are waiting to be made.

6. Involve Your Children

Invite them to help. Make a family cookbook, scrapbook, or playlist. Let them ask questions and share ideas. This helps them feel part of the process.

Remember: You are not just preparing your children for life without you—you are filling their hearts with a life shaped by your love.

🦋 Reflection | Prayer | Affirmation | Action
Creating Meaningful Memories

Reflection Questions
1. What everyday moments do you most want to remember?
2. What traditions do you want to begin or continue?
3. How do you want your children to feel when they think of you?

Affirmation
My love is alive in every memory, every tradition, every story I share.

Prayer
God, thank You for the gift of today. Help me savor these moments and create memories that will sustain my children with love and hope. Amen.

Action Steps
- Choose one tradition to start this month.
- Record a video message for your child.
- Begin a memory box or scrapbook together.

Chapter 4 : Creating a Peaceful Home Environment

A peaceful home can become a soft place to land—both for you and for your children.

As you prepare for the future, your physical environment can either add to your stress or help ease it.

Creating a comforting space isn't about having a perfect home—it's about cultivating an atmosphere that feels safe, loving, and steady.

In this chapter, you'll explore how decluttering with purpose, making your space more comforting, and gently preparing your children for change can all work together to create a home filled with peace.

Decluttering with Purpose

Clutter carries emotional weight. Each object tells a story, holds a memory, or represents an unspoken hope. Sorting through these things can feel overwhelming, but it can also be freeing.

Decluttering doesn't mean stripping your space of everything. It means surrounding yourself with what truly matters—what brings you comfort, beauty, and ease.

- Start small. Choose one drawer, one shelf, or one corner at a time.
- Decide what to keep, what to gift to loved ones, and what to let go.
- Consider creating a "legacy box" with keepsakes for your children—photos, letters, or special mementos that tell your story.

Making Your Space Comforting

When life feels uncertain, your surroundings can be a powerful source of calm.

Simple ways to create a soothing atmosphere:

- Soft lighting: Use lamps instead of overhead lights for a warm glow.
- Comfort items: Keep cozy blankets, favorite books, or meaningful objects within reach.
- Calming scents: Use essential oils or candles with gentle fragrances like lavender or vanilla.
- Quiet corners: Create a small spot for reflection, prayer, or rest.

Your home doesn't have to be magazine-perfect. It just needs to feel like yours.

Preparing Your Children for Change

As you declutter or update your home, involve your children gently. Change can be unsettling, especially if they sense what it means.

- Use simple, age-appropriate language to explain what you're doing.
- Invite them to choose keepsakes that matter to them.
- Reassure them that while some things will change, your love for them never will.

When children feel included, they feel more secure.

Reflection | Prayer | Affirmation | Action
Creating a Peaceful Home Environment

Reflection Questions
1. What items in my home bring me the most peace and comfort?
2. What could I let go of to create more space for calm and connection?
3. How can I involve my children in this process in a loving way?

Affirmation
My home is a place of love, peace, and gentle preparation. I am creating an environment that nurtures my spirit and comforts my children.

Prayer
God, Help me release what no longer serves me and make space for what matters most.

May my home be filled with Your peace and become a haven for my children as we walk this path together. Amen.

Action Steps

- Choose one area to declutter this week.
- Set aside meaningful keepsakes for your children.
- Add comforting touches to your space—a candle, a soft blanket, a family photo.
- Talk with your children about any changes in the home.
- Create a quiet corner for rest and reflection.

Part II: Understanding and Documenting Your Wishes

Chapter 5: Understanding End-of-Life Documents

> "Love prepares, even for the things we wish would never happen."

There's nothing easy about imagining your children or loved ones without you. But one of the most powerful, loving actions you can take is to prepare essential legal documents that clearly express your wishes and protect those you care about most.

Legal paperwork can feel overwhelming, but it's one of the clearest ways to ensure your family is protected and your desires are honored. This chapter simplifies the most important documents—wills, trusts, advance directives, guardianship designations, and powers of attorney—so you can make informed decisions with peace of mind.

By putting your plans in writing now, you give your family a precious gift: clarity and comfort when they'll need it most.

Reflection | Prayer | Affirmation | Action

Understanding End-of-Life Documents

Reflection Questions

1. What feelings come up for you as you think about creating these documents?
2. What do you most want to protect for your children or loved ones?
3. Who can you trust to help you carry out your wishes?

Affirmation

Preparing today is an act of love. My plans are a gift that will guide and protect my family.

Prayer

God, give me strength to make decisions that honor my life and care for the people I love.

Help me trust that these plans are an expression of my heart, not my fear. Amen.

Action Steps

- Make a list of which documents you already have and which ones you still need.
- Schedule a consultation with an estate planning attorney or trusted advisor.
- Write down the names of at least two people you would want to serve as guardians or decision-makers.

Chapter 6: What Is Estate Planning?

Estate planning is the intentional act of caring for your loved ones after you're gone—or if you can't speak for yourself.

While a will is foundational, true estate planning goes further. It means knowing what you have, deciding what you want to happen, and putting it all in writing so no one is left guessing or fighting.

Many people believe estate planning is only for the wealthy. The truth is, every family benefits from having a plan. Whether your assets are modest or complex, your wishes are equally important.

When you take the time to prepare, you remove burdens from your family and replace chaos with clarity. It's an act of love, stewardship, and faith.

Reflection | Prayer | Affirmation | Action

What Is Estate Planning?

Reflection Questions

1. Take a breath and reflect on what you've learned so far.
2. What have you avoided thinking about when it comes to your finances or personal affairs?
3. How does it feel to think about putting your wishes in writing?
4. What is one hope you have for your family after you're gone?

Affirmation

"I am preparing in love, not fear."

Prayer — A Prayer for Purposeful Preparation

God, help me to see this process not as morbid, but as sacred.

As I organize my affairs, remind me that I am creating peace for the people I love most.

Thank You for giving me the clarity and courage to prepare.

Guide my decisions so that my life—and my death—reflect Your love and provision. Amen.

Action Steps

- Make a list of every asset you own (home, accounts, valuables).
- Write down your debts and obligations.
- Review your beneficiary designations on retirement and investment accounts.
- Store this information safely and tell your executor where to find it.

Chapter 7: Which Legal Documents Do I Need?

Every estate plan should begin with a will—it clarifies who inherits your assets and ensures your wishes are honored.

But depending on your situation, you may also need additional documents:

- Trusts: Manage or protect assets for children or loved ones.
- Power of Attorney: Allows someone you trust to handle your finances if you become incapacitated.
- Healthcare Directive: Guides your medical care if you cannot speak for yourself.
- Beneficiary Designations: Ensure your accounts transfer quickly to the right people.

You don't have to complete everything at once. Estate planning is a process you can take one step at a time.

🕊 Reflection | Prayer | Affirmation | Action

Which Legal Documents Do I Need?

Reflection Questions

1. Which of these documents feels most urgent for your family?
2. Who do you trust to carry out your wishes?
3. How will having these documents in place bring you peace?

Affirmation

"My decisions today will protect my loved ones tomorrow."

Prayer — A Prayer for Wisdom in Choosing

Lord, as I decide who will speak for me and manage what I leave behind, grant me wisdom.

Show me who has the integrity and love to handle these responsibilities.

Help me release any fear of judgment, and act with confidence and clarity. Amen.

Action Steps

- Choose your executor and power of attorney.
- Download or request templates for each document.
- Meet with an attorney to finalize them.
- Review your beneficiary designations to ensure they match your will.

Chapter 8: Organizing and Storing Your Important Documents

"Clarity and order today create peace for tomorrow."

You've made important decisions about your care, assets, guardianship, and legacy.

Now it's time to make sure those decisions can be found and followed.

Organizing your documents is a practical act of love that saves your family from confusion or stress.

Whether you use a physical binder or a secure digital vault, your system should answer one essential question:

"If something happened to me today, could someone I trust step in and know what to do?"

Why Organization Matters

When documents are scattered or incomplete, it can delay decisions, create disputes, or even cause lost assets.

A well-organized plan helps:

- Your executor and loved ones find what they need quickly
- Prevent legal or probate complications
- Ensure your healthcare wishes are honored
- Protect your financial and digital legacy
- Provide peace of mind for you and your family

Key Documents to Collect and Organize

- Wills and Trusts
- Powers of Attorney (Financial and Medical)
- Advance Directives and Living Wills
- Life Insurance Policies
- Property Deeds and Vehicle Titles
- Financial Account Statements
- Debt and Loan Records
- Business Ownership Documents
- Tax Returns and Records
- Passwords and Digital Account Information
- Funeral Instructions and Letters to Loved Ones

Best Practices for Document Storage

1. Choose a Secure, Accessible Location

Use a fireproof safe, bank deposit box, or digital vault.

2. Make Copies

Keep both physical and digital versions.

3. Create an Inventory List

List all documents, their locations, and access details. Update yearly.

4. Review and Update Regularly

Life changes require document updates.

5. Communicate Your Plan

Let your executor or next of kin know where to find everything.

Adding a Personal Touch

Consider including letters, favorite scriptures, recipes, or blessings. These turn your binder or vault into a legacy of the heart—a reflection of your love, faith, and foresight.

When your loved ones open your files, they'll find not just paperwork—but peace, direction, and comfort.

🕊 Reflection | Prayer | Affirmation | Action

Organizing and Storing Your Important Documents

Reflection Questions

1. Who would need access to your documents if something happened tomorrow?
2. Do you prefer a physical binder, a digital vault, or both?
3. Have you told someone you trust where they are stored?
4. What personal touches could you include?

Affirmation

"My organization is a final act of love and kindness. I am creating peace and ease for those I cherish."

Prayer

Lord, help me gather the details of my life with care and intention. Give me the wisdom to prepare and the courage to share. Let my organization be a blessing and my legacy a reflection of Your peace. Amen.

Action Steps

- Choose your storage method (binder, vault, or both).
- Gather all essential documents in one place.
- Create a detailed inventory list.
- Share access with your executor or trusted loved ones.
- Schedule an annual review to update everything.
- Consider using a secure digital service for storage.

Chapter 9: Common Estate Planning Mistakes

Many people delay or avoid estate planning because it feels uncomfortable or intimidating.

But small mistakes can create major challenges later.

Here are some of the most common:

1. Not having a plan at all
2. Failing to communicate your wishes
3. Naming only one beneficiary
4. Forgetting about digital assets and accounts
5. Not updating your plan after major life changes

Avoiding these mistakes is an act of stewardship, responsibility, and love.

🐾 Reflection | Prayer | Affirmation | Action

Common Estate Planning Mistakes

Reflection Questions

1. Have I avoided planning out of fear or procrastination?
2. What is one simple step I can take today to bring clarity to my family?
3. How can I communicate my wishes with grace and confidence?

Affirmation

"I am capable of creating order and clarity."

Prayer

Dear God, help me take the first step without fear. Preparation is an expression of love.

Give me the strength to follow through and the humility to ask for help when needed.

Let my plans bring peace to my family. Amen.

Action Steps

- Commit to reviewing your plan annually.
- Make a list of all digital accounts and assign management instructions.
- Choose a backup beneficiary for every asset.
- Schedule a family conversation about your wishes.

Chapter 10: The Risks of Not Having an Estate Plan

If you pass away without a clear plan:

1. Your estate will go through probate court—a lengthy and costly process.
2. A judge, not your family, will decide who inherits your assets.
3. Your loved ones may experience unnecessary stress, confusion, or conflict.

Planning now means protecting them later. Estate planning isn't about fear—it's about faith, love, and responsible stewardship.

Reflection | Prayer | Affirmation | Action

The Risks of Not Having an Estate Plan

Reflection Questions

1. Who will be most affected if I don't have a clear plan?
2. How does it feel imagining my family having to guess my wishes?
3. What's one reason it's worth taking action today?

Affirmation

"I am choosing peace over procrastination."

Prayer — A Prayer for Motivation

God, give me the strength to do what I've been putting off.

Even though this work feels heavy, I trust You to guide my hands and my heart.

Help me remember that this preparation is a gift to the people I love. Amen.

Action Steps

- Start or update your will.
- Create a list of all assets, debts, and accounts.
- Share your plans with your executor or trusted family member.
- Keep all documents in a secure but accessible place.

Part III: Guardianship, Care, and Special Considerations

Financial Planning for a Lasting Legacy

Chapter 11: Guardianship and Care Decisions

"Your love can keep guiding your children, even when you cannot."

Naming guardians for your children is one of the most important decisions you can make.

It ensures they will be cared for by someone who knows them, loves them, and shares your values.

In this chapter, you'll reflect on:

- Who you trust to raise your children if you cannot.
- How to document your wishes in a will or guardianship appointment.
- How to create a letter of intent or care plan to guide future caregivers.
- Special considerations for single parents or children with special needs.

These choices are tender, but they are also powerful. They say to your children:

You will always be protected.

🕊 Reflection | Prayer | Affirmation | Action

Guardianship and Care Decisions

Reflection Questions
1. Who shares your values and would honor your wishes for your children?
2. What qualities matter most to you in a guardian?
3. What hopes or traditions would you want your children's caregivers to continue?

Affirmation
I am choosing protection, love, and security for my children. My decisions are a legacy of care.

Prayer
God, please guide my heart as I choose the people who will care for my children.

Give me wisdom to trust that my love will keep surrounding them, even when I cannot. Amen.

Action Steps
- Write down a shortlist of potential guardians and backup guardians.
- Have an honest conversation with your chosen guardians about your wishes.

- Begin drafting a letter of intent to share your hopes, values, and guidance for your children's care.

Every page, every plan, every signature is proof of your love.

You are not just organizing paperwork—you are creating peace, security, and clarity for the people who matter most.

Chapter 12: Planning for Guardianship of Minor Children

"Who will hold their hands when you can't?"

One of the most heart-wrenching questions for any parent facing serious illness or the unknown future is: Who will care for my children if I'm not here?

Guardianship planning is about more than just naming a person on paper—it's about choosing someone who will love, protect, and raise your children according to your values and hopes.

Having a clear guardianship plan brings peace to you and security to your children.

Why Guardianship Planning Matters

Without a legal guardianship designation, the court decides who cares for your children. This can lead to delays, confusion, and even family conflict during an already painful time.

By choosing your guardian, you ensure your children are cared for by someone you trust and who understands your parenting style and your family's unique needs.

Who Can Be a Guardian?

A guardian can be:

- A close family member (grandparent, aunt, uncle, sibling)
- A trusted friend or mentor
- A godparent or someone who shares your values

When choosing, consider:

- Their willingness and ability to care for your children
- Their parenting style and values
- Their proximity and lifestyle (can they provide stability?)
- Their health and age
- Their financial ability and support system

How to Set Up Guardianship

Talk to Potential Guardians

- Discuss your hopes and expectations, and make sure they are willing to take on this important role.

Legal Documentation

- Appoint your chosen guardian in your will or a separate guardianship document. This ensures your wishes are legally recognized.

Backup Guardians

- Name at least one alternate guardian in case your first choice can't serve.

Provide Guidance

- Consider writing letters or notes to your guardians about your children's routines, preferences, medical needs, education, and discipline.

Preparing Your Children

Depending on their age and understanding, gently prepare your children for the possibility of a new guardian.

Keep communication open and reassure them that they will be cared for and loved.

🦬 Reflection | Prayer | Affirmation | Action

Planning for Guardianship of Minor Children

Reflection

1. Who embodies the love and values I want to pass to my children?
2. How can I ease my children's transition by preparing their guardian ahead of time?
3. What hopes do I want to share with the person caring for my children?

Affirmation

I am a loving parent who plans with courage and clarity. My children's future is bright and protected.

Prayer

God, bless the hands that will care for my children.

Give them strength, wisdom, and love to guide and nurture as I would. Amen.

Action Steps

- Have a heartfelt conversation with your chosen guardian(s).
- Legally appoint guardians in your will or legal documents.

- Create a guardian letter with important information about your children.
- Review and update guardianship plans regularly, especially after major life changes.

Chapter 13: Planning for Loved Ones with Special Needs

Caring for someone with special needs or vulnerabilities is one of the greatest acts of love and commitment.

Whether you're the parent of a child with disabilities, caring for an aging parent, or supporting a loved one living with mental illness or chronic health challenges, your planning can provide them with safety, dignity, and continuity of care when you're no longer able to be there.

This chapter guides you through the key steps and considerations to create a plan that honors their unique needs.

Why Specialized Planning Matters

Traditional estate planning may not address the complexities that come with special needs or vulnerable situations.

Without careful preparation:

- Your loved one's eligibility for public benefits (like Medicaid or Supplemental Security Income) could be jeopardized.
- There may be no clear instructions for their care, housing, and medical decisions.

- Family members might disagree or feel unprepared to step in.

When you take time now to plan intentionally, you help avoid confusion, protect essential benefits, and make sure your loved one continues to receive the support they need.

Key Steps to Protect and Provide

1. Identify Their Needs

Make a clear list of:

- Medical conditions and medications
- Daily care routines
- Educational supports
- Behavioral or emotional considerations
- Important providers and contacts

This will become part of your care plan.

2. Appoint a Guardian or Conservator

Consider who you trust to make decisions if you are incapacitated or pass away. You can:

- Name a guardian (for personal and medical decisions)
- Appoint a conservator (to manage finances)
- Include backups in case your first choice is unable to serve.

3. Establish a Special Needs Trust

A special needs trust (sometimes called a supplemental needs trust) allows you to set aside funds to enhance your loved one's quality of life without affecting eligibility for means-tested benefits.

These funds can be used for:

1. Therapies not covered by insurance
2. Personal care assistants
3. Specialized equipment
4. Education and recreation

Tip: Work with an estate planning attorney who specializes in special needs trusts to ensure compliance with state and federal laws.

4. Draft a Letter of Intent

While not a legal document, a Letter of Intent provides vital information about your loved one's preferences, routines, and care history. It helps future caregivers understand their personality and needs.

Include:

- Daily schedule
- Food preferences
- Communication styles
- Behavioral triggers
- Religious or cultural practices

Keep it updated annually.

5. Review Beneficiary Designations

Never leave assets directly to your loved one through life insurance or retirement accounts if it could compromise their benefits. Instead, direct these assets to the special needs trust.

6. Build a Support Network

Talk with family, close friends, and professionals about your plans. Share your vision for your loved one's future and ask for their commitment to be part of the care team if needed.

Common Mistakes to Avoid

1. Leaving an outright inheritance to a person receiving public benefits
2. Failing to update beneficiary designations
3. Not appointing successor trustees or guardians
4. Keeping plans secret or unshared with your support network

Reflection | Prayer | Affirmation | Action
Planning for Loved Ones with Special Needs

Reflection Questions

Take a quiet moment and consider:

1. What is my deepest hope for my loved one's future when I'm no longer here?
2. Who in my life could step into a caregiving or supportive role?
3. What information would help someone understand and care for my loved one?
4. How can I start this planning process without feeling overwhelmed?

Affirmation

My love and care will continue beyond my lifetime. I am creating a foundation of security, dignity, and compassion for those who need me most.

Prayer

Dear God,

You know the tender places of my heart where worry and love meet.

Please give me strength, wisdom, and courage to plan for my loved one's needs.

Help me trust that You will watch over them and guide those who step into my place.

May every detail of this plan reflect Your love and my devotion. Amen.

Action Steps

Start with one small, clear action:

- Make a list of your loved one's medical, personal, and daily care needs.
- Schedule a consultation with a special needs planning attorney.
- Identify and speak with potential guardians about your wishes.
- Create or update beneficiary designations to direct assets to a trust, not directly to your loved one.
- Write a Letter of Intent describing your loved one's routines, preferences, and supports.
- Review your plan annually to keep it current.

Planning for your loved one's future can feel heavy, but it is an act of profound love.

You are building a legacy of care that will outlast your own lifetime—a gift of security and dignity that is priceless.

Chapter 14: Choosing a Power of Attorney and Healthcare Proxy

"Who will speak for you when you can't speak for yourself?"

This is one of the most important—and often most emotional—decisions you'll make in your estate planning journey.

A power of attorney gives someone you trust the legal authority to act on your behalf if you become incapacitated. A healthcare proxy (also called a medical power of attorney) allows someone to make medical decisions if you can't.

While none of us likes to imagine being unable to speak or act for ourselves, naming these decision-makers protects your dignity, your family, and your wishes.

Why This Matters

When an unexpected crisis happens, your loved ones will already be overwhelmed. If you don't have these documents in place, the courts could end up deciding who will make decisions for you—and it might not be the person you'd choose.

By setting this up now, you are giving your family the gift of clarity and peace.

What Is a Power of Attorney?

A durable power of attorney (POA) allows someone you trust (your "agent") to manage your finances and legal affairs if you're unable to do so.

This includes:

- Paying your bills
- Handling your bank accounts
- Managing investments
- Buying or selling property
- Filing taxes

You can make the POA as broad or as limited as you like.

What Is a Healthcare Proxy?

A healthcare proxy gives someone you trust the authority to make medical decisions if you're unconscious or unable to communicate.

This person can:

- Talk with your doctors
- Decide about treatments
- Carry out your healthcare wishes

You can also create an Advance Directive, which clearly states your preferences about life support, resuscitation, and other critical care decisions.

Who Should You Choose?

This is not just about who you love—it's about who is capable, calm, and committed to honoring your wishes.

Consider someone who:

- Understands your values
- Is comfortable making tough decisions
- Will advocate for you without hesitation
- Can handle stress without being overwhelmed

Often, this is a spouse, adult child, close friend, or trusted advisor.

How to Set It Up

Talk to the Person First

- Make sure they're willing and able to take on this responsibility.

Complete the Legal Documents

- Use the templates in this kit or consult an estate attorney to draft the POA and healthcare proxy forms.

Be Specific

- Clearly outline any limits or special instructions.

Sign and Notarize

- Many states require notarization and witnesses.

Distribute Copies

Keep originals in a safe place, and give copies to:

- Your agent/proxy
- Your healthcare providers
- A backup agent (if you have one)

🦋 Reflection | Prayer | Affirmation | Action

Choosing a Power of Attorney and Healthcare Proxy

Reflection

1. Who do I trust most to carry out my wishes?
2. What values matter most to me in healthcare and financial decisions?
3. How can I ease my family's burden by being clear now?

Affirmation

I am prepared.

I am protected.

My voice will be honored, even when I cannot speak it myself.

Prayer

Lord, grant me wisdom as I choose the people who will stand in my place.

Help me trust that I am not leaving my care to chance but to hands guided by Your grace.

Amen.

Action Steps

- Use the Power of Attorney and Healthcare Proxy templates in this kit.
- Talk with your chosen agents to confirm their understanding and agreement.
- Store signed copies in a safe place and share them with key people.
- Review these documents every 1–2 years to ensure they still reflect your wishes.

Part IV: Financial Planning and Protecting Your Legacy

Chapter 15: Building Your Financial Footprint — Protecting Your Children's Future

"Money doesn't buy peace—but planning does."

Finances can feel overwhelming, especially when you're managing parenting, bills, and emotions all at once.

But here's a truth to hold on to: you don't need to be wealthy to leave a strong foundation for your children.

What matters most is clarity, intention, and a thoughtful plan.

A simple, future-focused financial plan can bring peace to your present and security for your children's future.

This chapter guides you to take inventory of your assets and debts, create a legacy-minded budget, and choose trusted people to carry out your wishes.

Tips to building your financial blueprint

1. Take Inventory of What You Have

Many moms don't realize how much they've built already—whether it's a savings account, a retirement fund, or even sentimental valuables. Your financial footprint includes everything of value you own, like:

- Cash and savings (bank accounts, emergency funds, digital wallets)
- Investments (stocks, bonds, retirement accounts like 401(k)s or IRAs)
- Property (homes, vehicles, land)
- Insurance policies (life insurance, HSAs, long-term care)
- Personal property (jewelry, heirlooms)
- Business assets (if you own or co-own a business)

Create a simple list or spreadsheet to visualize your assets. Don't worry about exact values at first — just get it all down.

2. Understand Your Debts

Knowing what you owe is just as important. While debts aren't passed directly to your children, they affect your estate and the distribution of your assets. Common debts include:

- Mortgage or rent
- Credit card balances
- Personal loans

- Student loans (some may be discharged at death)
- Car loans
- Medical bills

Having this clear picture can help you make decisions now to reduce the burden on your family later.

3. Create a Future-Focused Budget

Budgeting isn't just about paying bills today — it's about making space for your legacy.

Think about:

- Immediate needs (funeral costs, final medical bills)
- Short-term support (helping your children with housing, groceries, childcare)
- Long-term growth (college savings, trust funds, inheritance growth)

Even small contributions now — like setting aside $20 a month — can build meaningful support over time.

4. Choose Financial Guardians Wisely

Decide who will manage your estate and your children's inheritance. This might be called a Successor Trustee (if you have a trust) or a Personal Representative (if you have a will). These people handle debts, distribute assets, and fulfill your wishes.

Also consider:

- Executor: Handles your will and estate distribution
- Financial guardian: Manages money for minor children
- Power of attorney: Handles your finances if you're incapacitated

Choose responsible, trustworthy people who understand and honor your values.

5. Make It Official

- Document your wishes clearly by:
- Writing a will (even a simple one)
- Naming beneficiaries on all accounts
- Setting up transfer-on-death/payable-on-death designations
- Considering a trust if you want more control over asset use

You can use online resources or a lawyer—whatever fits your situation best.

6. Teach Your Children (as Age Allows)

Financial legacy isn't just money—it's also wisdom. Teach your children about money at a level they can understand:

- For young kids: "We save money to take care of each other."
- For teens: Show them how budgeting works or walk them through your bank app.
- For adults: Share where to find important documents and financial information.

Talking about money now helps prepare them to carry your legacy forward with confidence.

Reflection | Prayer | Affirmation | Action

Building Your Financial Footprint — Protecting Your Children's Future

Reflection Questions

1. What financial assets and resources do I currently have that I might be overlooking?
2. How do I want my money to support my children's future?
3. Who do I trust to manage my financial affairs with care and responsibility?
4. What fears or concerns about money can I face today with honesty and clarity?

Affirmation

I am capable of creating a clear, loving financial plan that protects my family and reflects my values. My intentional actions today bring peace and security for those I love.

Prayer

Dear God,

Grant me wisdom and peace as I organize my finances.

Help me trust Your guidance and to act with courage and love.

Bless the plans I make so they protect and nurture my family in every season. Amen.

Action Steps

- List all assets and debts to gain full clarity on your financial footprint.
- Create a budget that includes immediate, short-term, and long-term needs for your children's care.
- Identify and write down trusted individuals for executor, financial guardian, and power of attorney roles.
- Begin drafting or updating your will and beneficiary designations using online tools or legal help.
- Start age-appropriate conversations with your children about money and legacy.

Chapter 16: Inheritance Planning with Intention — Leaving More Than Money

"Leaving money is one thing. Leaving a plan for it is love."

When we think about inheritance, it's easy to focus only on the dollars and cents. But what truly matters is how you leave it. As a mother, your love is in the everyday moments — the hugs, the sacrifices, the tough conversations.

Planning your inheritance is another act of love, one that brings peace and security long after you're gone.

This chapter guides you through the practical and emotional layers of inheritance planning, helping you pass on not just assets, but your intentions, wisdom, and care.

Inheritance planning tips
1. Start with the End in Mind
Before paperwork and legal jargon, ask yourself:
- What do I want my legacy to do?
- Support my children through college?
- Leave a safety net for future generations?

- Give to a cause close to my heart?

Write down your goals, even if rough — they'll guide your legal and financial decisions.

2. Wills vs. Trusts: Know the Difference

Will: A legal document stating who gets what, but must go through probate — a slow, public process.

Trust: Avoids probate, offers privacy and control. A revocable living trust is a common family tool.

Trusts can:

- Distribute funds gradually (good for young children)
- Protect assets from creditors or divorce
- Ensure responsible money management for minors or vulnerable adults

Work with an estate planning attorney to find the right option for your family. The investment in time and money now pays off in peace later.

3. Beneficiaries: Choose with Care

Assets like life insurance, retirement funds, and bank accounts often pass outside wills through beneficiary designations. Keeping these up-to-date is vital to avoid confusion or unintended heirs.

- Regularly review beneficiaries on all accounts
- Update after major life changes (divorce, remarriage, births)

- List contingent beneficiaries as backups
- Avoid naming minor children directly — use a trust or custodian instead

This prevents family conflicts and helps your trustee distribute assets smoothly.

4. The Power of Life Insurance

Life insurance can replace income, pay debts, or give your children a strong financial start. Term life insurance is affordable and straightforward.

Ask yourself:

- Is my coverage enough to support my family's lifestyle for several years?
- Who will manage the payout for minor children?
- Does the money go directly to a person or into a trust?
- Even a modest policy, used intentionally, makes a big difference.

5. Avoiding Common Pitfalls

- No plan at all: Without a will or trust, state law decides, which may not match your wishes.
- Outdated documents: Life changes — so should your plan. Review after major events.

- Too much too soon: A lump sum inheritance at 18 can overwhelm. Consider staged distributions or trusts with conditions.

6. Leave a Letter, Not Just Legalities

Your legacy is also deeply personal.

Write a legacy letter sharing your values, hopes, and memories.

Money is useful, but your words can comfort and guide your children in ways no dollar ever could.

By planning your inheritance with intention, you give your children one last gift: clarity in grief and a future shaped by your love.

🐾 Reflection | Prayer | Affirmation | Action

Inheritance Planning with Intention — Leaving More Than Money

Reflection Questions

2. What are my most important goals for the legacy I leave?
3. How do wills, trusts, and beneficiary designations fit into my family's needs?
4. Who are the trustworthy people I can count on to carry out my wishes?
5. What fears or concerns about inheritance planning do I need to face?

Affirmation

I am creating a thoughtful, clear inheritance plan that reflects my love and protects my family's future. My intentions guide every decision I make.

Prayer

God,

Grant me wisdom and peace as I prepare my inheritance plan.

Help me to leave behind more than assets — a legacy of love, care, and clear guidance.

Strengthen me to make decisions that honor my family and my values. Amen.

Action Steps

- Write down your key inheritance goals and intentions.
- Decide whether a will, trust, or both best serve your family's needs.
- Review and update all beneficiary designations on your accounts.
- Evaluate your life insurance coverage and beneficiary arrangements.
- Schedule a consultation with an estate planning attorney.
- Draft a legacy letter to share your values and hopes with your children.
- Review your estate plan regularly and after major life changes.

Chapter 17: Creating or Updating Your Will

"Your will is your voice—use it to speak love and clarity into your children's future."

A will is the foundation of your estate plan. It's the document that ensures your wishes are known, your assets are distributed according to your values, and—most importantly—your children are protected.

Without a will, the state decides what happens, and those decisions may not reflect what's best for your family.

Creating a will isn't just about money—it's about peace, clarity, and intentional love.

What to Include in Your Will

Your Children's Guardian

- Name the person(s) you trust to raise your children if you're no longer here.
- Have a conversation with them ahead of time to make sure they're willing and able.

Your Executor

- Choose someone who is responsible and trustworthy to carry out your final wishes.

- This person will handle distributing your assets, paying bills, and managing your estate.

How You Want Your Assets Divided

- List specific gifts (such as heirlooms, cars, or savings) to specific people.
- You can also list percentages (e.g., "split evenly between my children") or create a trust.

Any Final Wishes

- This can include your funeral preferences, spiritual wishes, or personal messages to your children or loved ones.

Will vs. Living Trust: What's the Difference?

A will is read and acted upon after your death and often goes through probate (court involvement).

A revocable living trust, which we'll discuss in the next chapter, can avoid probate and provide more flexibility.

Still, everyone should have a will—even if they also create a trust.

What Happens Without a Will?

- The court decides who raises your children.
- Your estate may be delayed in probate.

- Your assets may not go to the people you intended.
- Your family may face stress, confusion, or even conflict.

Don't leave it up to chance. Your will is one of the most powerful documents you can create to protect your family's future.

🕊 Reflection | Prayer | Affirmation | Action

Creating or Updating Your Will

Reflection

1. What legacy do I want to leave behind, not just in things, but in love?
2. Who would raise my children with values closest to mine?
3. What fears come up when I think about writing a will—and what would bring me peace?

Affirmation

My will is an act of love. I am preparing with courage, not fear.

Prayer

God, give me the courage to face these sacred decisions with clarity and love.

Let this process be one of peace, not fear.

Remind me that I'm not just planning for death—but building a future of protection, dignity, and love for my children.

Let every choice I make reflect Your wisdom and my heart. Amen.

Action Steps

- Use the "Last Will and Testament Template" in this kit to begin drafting your will.
- Make a list of people you trust as guardians or executors.
- Write down specific gifts or personal notes you want to leave.
- Speak with a lawyer or estate planner to finalize and notarize your will.
- Store it in a safe, accessible place and let someone know where it is.

Chapter 18: Setting Up a Living Trust

"Build a bridge—not a burden—for those you love."

A living trust is one of the most powerful tools in estate planning.

1. It allows you to transfer your assets privately, quickly, and with fewer complications—especially compared to probate.
2. It also gives you more control over how and when your assets are distributed, which can be especially helpful if your children are still young or if you want to protect a loved one with special needs, addiction, or financial instability.

A will says what you want.

A trust makes it happen—with fewer delays and more protection.

What Is a Living Trust?

A revocable living trust is a legal document that lets you place assets (like your house, bank accounts, or personal property) into a trust during your lifetime.

You still control it and can make changes at any time.

After your death, your appointed trustee manages and distributes those assets according to your instructions—without going through probate.

Benefits of a Living Trust

- Avoids probate court (saving time, money, and stress)
- Keeps your financial matters private
- Protects your children from managing large inheritances too young
- Allows for ongoing support for a loved one with special needs
- Gives flexibility to manage your affairs if you become incapacitated

Key Roles in Your Trust

1. Grantor – That's you. You create and fund the trust.
2. Trustee – The person who manages the trust. You can be your own trustee while you're living, and name a backup (successor) for when you're gone or incapacitated.
3. Beneficiaries – The people (like your children) who receive the assets from the trust.
4. Successor Trustee – The person who takes over managing the trust if you pass away or become unable to continue.

What Can You Put in a Trust?

- Your home or other real estate
- Bank accounts
- Vehicles
- Investments or retirement accounts
- Life insurance
- Business interests
- Family heirlooms or personal items
- Anything of value you want to pass on smoothly

How to Create a Living Trust

- Write the Trust Document
- You can use the template included in this book or work with an estate attorney for a custom version.
- Name the Trustee and Beneficiaries
- Choose someone you trust deeply and who's capable of managing important decisions.
- Transfer Ownership of Assets into the Trust
- This is the most important (and most overlooked) step. You must retitle your property into the name of the trust. Otherwise, it's not covered.
- Keep It Updated
- Review and revise your trust as your circumstances, relationships, or assets change.

When Should You Use a Trust Instead of a Will?

- You want to avoid probate for a home or property
- You have a child with special needs
- You want to provide structured payments (not a lump sum)
- You want privacy
- You own property in multiple states
- You're worried about family conflict or confusion

Most people will need both a will and a trust to ensure full coverage and peace of mind.

🦋 Reflection | Prayer | Affirmation | Action

Setting Up a Living Trust

Reflection

1. Who do I trust to manage my estate with wisdom and care?
2. What legacy do I want to pass on—not just wealth, but peace and protection?
3. Am I ready to create something that brings clarity, not confusion, for my family?

Affirmation

I am building a plan that brings peace, not pain. My trust reflects my values and protects my family.

Prayer

God, as I plan for the future, help me make choices with clarity and courage.

Let this trust be a sacred bridge that carries my love, my values, and my provision to the people I care about most.

Thank You for giving me wisdom in every detail. Amen.

Action Steps

- Use the "Revocable Living Trust Template" in this kit to begin creating your trust.
- Choose your successor trustee carefully—someone organized and trustworthy.
- Begin transferring property titles and assets into the trust's name.
- Talk with a legal or financial advisor to ensure everything is legally sound.
- Keep a copy of the trust with your important documents, and share its location with your trustee.

Chapter 19: Planning for Your Business and Succession

"Protecting your legacy and securing the future of what you've built."

If you own a business, your estate plan must include thoughtful preparation to ensure your work continues to thrive after you're gone.

Whether it's a small family business, a sole proprietorship, or a growing enterprise, succession planning is vital to protect your legacy and provide stability for your employees and loved ones.

Why Business Succession Planning Matters

Without a clear plan, your business may face disruption, legal battles, or even closure after your death or incapacity. Succession planning allows you to:

- Maintain business continuity
- Provide for your family financially
- Minimize conflicts among heirs or partners
- Preserve jobs and client relationships
- Optimize tax and legal outcomes

Key Steps in Business Succession Planning

Identify Your Goals

What do you want to happen to your business? Do you want it to be sold, passed down to family, or managed by partners or employees? Your plan should reflect your values and vision.

Choose Your Successor(s)

Select the person or people you trust to take over your business. This could be a family member, business partner, key employee, or even an outside buyer.

Create a Succession Plan Document

This formal document outlines how ownership and management will transfer. It should include timelines, training plans, and any conditions for the transfer.

Legal and Financial Planning

Work with professionals to set up buy-sell agreements, update business ownership documents, and address tax implications.

Communicate Your Plan

Sharing your succession plan with key stakeholders helps prevent surprises and conflicts. Open communication builds trust and ensures smoother transitions.

✦ Reflection | Prayer | Affirmation | Action
Planning for Your Business and Succession

Reflection
1. What does my business mean to me and my family?
2. Who do I trust to carry on my vision and values?
3. How can I prepare them to succeed when the time comes?

Affirmation
I am securing the future of my business with clarity, care, and purpose.

Prayer
Creator of all endeavors, bless the work of my hands and heart.

Guide those who will carry my business forward with wisdom and integrity. Amen.

Action Steps
- Clarify your goals for your business's future.
- Identify and prepare your successor(s).
- Work with an attorney to draft or update a formal succession plan.

- Review and update business ownership documents and agreements.
- Consult financial and tax professionals for optimal planning.
- Communicate your plan with key people involved in your business.
- Schedule regular reviews of your succession plan as your business evolves.

Part V: Digital Assets, Communication, and Maintenance

Chapter 20: Managing Digital Assets and Your Online Legacy

When we think about what we leave behind, we often picture our homes, finances, and treasured keepsakes. But in today's world, your digital presence is part of your legacy too. This chapter will help you make a plan for your online accounts, social media, and digital memories.

What Are Digital Assets?

Digital assets are anything stored electronically or accessible online.

They include:

- Financial Accounts: Online banking, PayPal, investment accounts
- Social Media: Facebook, Instagram, Twitter, TikTok
- Email Accounts: Personal and work email
- Cloud Storage: Google Drive, Dropbox, iCloud
- Subscriptions: Streaming services, shopping accounts
- Domain Names and Websites
- Digital Photos and Videos

Without clear instructions, your loved ones might struggle to access or close these accounts.

Why It Matters

Leaving a plan protects your privacy, preserves memories, and reduces stress for your family. It also prevents identity theft and ensures your wishes are respected.

Steps to Organize Your Digital Legacy

1. Make an Inventory

Write a list of:

- All your online accounts
- Usernames and passwords (store securely)
- Subscription services
- Devices (laptops, tablets, phones)

Consider using a password manager to keep this information updated and safe.

2. Decide What You Want Done

For each account, consider:

- Should it be closed or memorialized?
- Should photos and files be saved?
- Who should have access?

For example:

Facebook allows you to assign a legacy contact or have your account deleted.

Google offers an Inactive Account Manager to share data if you stop using your account.

3. Name a Digital Executor

In many states, you can name someone to manage your digital affairs. This person will carry out your wishes regarding online accounts and assets.

Include this in your will or estate plan. Make sure they have instructions on where to find your login information.

4. Store Information Securely

Keep your digital asset list:

- In a safe place (fireproof box, secure file)
- With your attorney
- In a password manager
- With your estate planning documents

Never write down passwords in an obvious place without protection.

5. Communicate Your Plan

Talk to your trusted person about:

1. Where to find your list
2. What you want to happen to your accounts
3. How to handle photos and personal content

This conversation doesn't have to be complicated—it just needs to happen.

Special Considerations

- Photos & Videos: Decide who should inherit your digital albums.
- Business Accounts: If you run a business, leave clear instructions for social media, websites, and client files.
- Online Revenue: Accounts generating income (YouTube, Etsy, Patreon) should be included in your estate plan.

Managing your digital legacy is an act of love and responsibility. You're making sure your story, your memories, and your values are protected and honored.

You don't have to do it all in one day—start with one account and build from there.

🕊 Reflection | Prayer | Affirmation | Action

Managing Digital Assets and Your Online Legacy

Reflection Questions

Take a moment to reflect on these questions before you start organizing your digital legacy:

1. Which of my online accounts hold memories or important information I'd want my loved ones to have?
2. How would I feel if my accounts were left unmanaged or became vulnerable to misuse after I'm gone?
3. Who do I trust to carry out my wishes regarding my digital presence?
4. What small step could I take today to feel more at peace about my online legacy?

Affirmation

My memories are valuable, my story matters, and I have the power to protect and honor them.

Each step I take brings clarity and peace to those I love.

Prayer

Dear God,

Thank You for the gift of this life and the connections I've built. Help me to organize my digital world with wisdom and care.

Give me the strength to make decisions that reflect my heart and protect my loved ones. May my online legacy be a testimony of love, faith, and purpose. Amen.

Action Steps

Here are simple, concrete steps you can take this week:

- Make a list of your most important digital accounts (email, banking, social media).
- Decide what you'd like done with each account—memorialize, transfer, or delete.
- Choose a trusted person to be your digital executor and communicate your wishes with them.
- Store your login details securely in a password manager or safe place, and let your digital executor know how to access them.
- Schedule time once a year to update your digital inventory and confirm your plans still reflect your wishes.

Chapter 21: Updating and Maintaining Your Estate Plan

"Your plan grows with your life — keep it current, keep it strong."

Creating an estate plan is a powerful step toward peace of mind, but it's not a "set it and forget it" task. Life changes, laws evolve, and your priorities may shift over time.

To ensure your plan continues to protect your loved ones and honor your wishes, regular updates and maintenance are essential.

Why Updating Matters

Your estate plan is a living document. Without updates, it can become outdated, causing confusion or unintended consequences for those you care about.

Regular review helps you:

- Reflect your current family situation and relationships
- Account for new assets or changes in finances
- Adapt to changes in tax laws or state regulations

- Include new wishes for healthcare or guardianship
- Avoid disputes by clarifying unclear provisions

When to Review Your Estate Plan

Check in on your plan at least once every 1–3 years, or whenever you experience major life events such as:

- Marriage or divorce
- Birth or adoption of a child or grandchild
- Death of a beneficiary, executor, or guardian
- Significant changes in financial status (inheritance, sale of property, new business)
- Changes in tax laws or estate regulations
- Moving to a new state or country
- Changes in health or medical wishes
- Desire to support a new charity or cause

How to Maintain Your Plan

Keep Your Documents Organized

- Store all estate planning documents in a secure but accessible place. Ensure trusted individuals know where to find them.

Communicate Updates

- Share any changes with your family, executor, trustees, and advisors. Clear communication prevents surprises.

Consult Professionals

- Work with your estate attorney, financial planner, or tax advisor to make necessary adjustments and ensure legal compliance.

Review Beneficiary Designations

- Double-check that beneficiary information on life insurance, retirement accounts, and other assets matches your plan.

Document Changes Clearly

- Use codicils, amendments, or restatements as needed. Keep signed, dated copies with original documents.

🦋 Reflection | Prayer | Affirmation | Action

Updating and Maintaining Your Estate Plan

Reflection

1. When was the last time I reviewed my estate plan?
2. Have any recent life changes made updates necessary?
3. Who else needs to be informed about my plan?

Affirmation

I maintain my estate plan with care and clarity, creating security and peace for those I love.

Prayer

Dear God, Guide me with wisdom to keep my plans current and true, that my loved ones may always be cared for and my wishes honored.

Give me the discernment to know when to adjust and the courage to act. Amen.

Action Steps

- Schedule a yearly or biennial review of your estate plan.
- Note any recent changes in your life that may affect your plan.
- Contact your estate planning attorney or financial advisor for guidance.
- Update beneficiary designations as needed.
- Share updates and document changes clearly with trusted individuals.

Chapter 22: Estate Plan Annual Review Checklist

Use this checklist each year—or whenever a major life event occurs—to ensure your estate plan is up-to-date and still serves your family.

Personal Information

- Have you moved to a new state or country?
- Have your contact details changed?

Family & Relationships

- Have you married, divorced, or entered a new partnership?
- Have you had a child, adopted, or gained new dependents?
- Has any beneficiary, executor, trustee, or guardian passed away?
- Have any relationships changed in ways that affect your wishes?

Assets & Finances

- Have you bought or sold real estate?
- Have you started, sold, or closed a business?
- Have you inherited or gifted significant assets?

- Have your investments or insurance policies changed?

Legal & Healthcare

- Do your healthcare directives still reflect your wishes?
- Do you need to update your HIPAA authorization?
- Are your powers of attorney still appropriate?
- Has tax law changed in a way that affects your plan?

Charitable Wishes

- Do you want to add or remove charities in your plan?
- Are your legacy gifts still aligned with your values?

Beneficiary Designation Review Worksheet

Instructions: Review all accounts with beneficiary designations outside your will or trust (such as life insurance, retirement plans, pensions, and bank accounts).

Ensure the beneficiaries align with your estate plan.

Account or Policy	Institution	Primary Beneficiary	Secondary Beneficiary	Notes
Example: 401(k)	ABC Retirement	Jane Doe	Sam Doe	

Document Organization Log

Keep track of where your most important documents are stored and who has access.

Document	Date Last Updated	Location	Who Has Access?
1. Will			
2. Revocable Living Trust			
3. Powers of Attorney			
4. Advance Directive			
5. HIPAA Authorization			
6. Life Insurance Policies			
7. Deeds & Titles			
8. Business Documents			
9. Funeral Wishes			

Other

Tip: Make a copy of this log for your executor or trustee.

Chapter 23: Estate Plan Update Action Plan

Whenever your review indicates updates are needed, use this plan to stay organized and intentional.

Update Steps

1. What needs updating?

    Example: Add new grandchild as beneficiary.

2. Why?

    Example: Child born in June.

3. Who do I need to contact?

    Attorney, financial advisor, insurance agent, etc.

4. When will I complete this?

    Include a realistic completion date.

5. How will I share the updates?

    Inform your executor, trustee, or family members.

Action Plan Log

Task Person Responsible Deadline Notes

_____

Reflection Prompts

Use these journal questions annually:

1. Does my estate plan still reflect my core values and goals?
2. Have there been any significant life events in my family?
3. Who do I trust most to help manage my affairs if I am unable?
4. Do I feel at peace with the current plans, or is there something I've been avoiding updating?

Chapter 24: Communicating Your Plan with Loved Ones

"Clear communication is the greatest gift you can give your family."

You've done the hard work of planning—setting goals, organizing documents, and making decisions. Now it's time to share your plan with those who will carry it forward.

Open and honest conversations about your wishes provide clarity, prevent misunderstandings, and offer your loved ones peace of mind.

Why Communication Matters

When your family knows your plans, they are less likely to feel lost or overwhelmed during an already difficult time. Clear communication:

- Prevents confusion and conflict
- Builds trust and understanding
- Empowers your loved ones to act confidently
- Honors your values and intentions
- Creates a legacy of openness and love

Tips for Sharing Your Plan

Choose the Right Time and Place

- Find a calm, private moment to discuss your estate plan. Make sure everyone feels safe to ask questions and share feelings.

Be Clear and Compassionate

- Explain your decisions simply and lovingly. Emphasize that your plan is about protecting and providing for them.

Introduce Your Executor and Trustees

- Ensure the people you've chosen to manage your estate or care for your children understand their roles and responsibilities.

Provide Access to Documents

- Let your loved ones know where to find your important documents and who to contact if they need help.

Prepare for Emotional Reactions

- These conversations can bring up strong feelings. Be patient, and encourage open dialogue.

Document Your Conversations

- Consider writing down key points or recording discussions, so there's a clear record of your wishes.

Keep the Conversation Ongoing

- Estate planning is not a one-time talk. Revisit your plan and update your family as needed—especially after major life changes.

🕮 Reflection | Prayer | Affirmation | Action

Communicating Your Plan with Loved Ones

Reflection Questions

1. Have I shared my plan with those who need to know?
2. Am I prepared to answer their questions honestly and with kindness?
3. How can I continue to keep communication open and supportive?

Affirmation

I communicate my plans clearly and lovingly, creating peace and confidence for my family.

Prayer

Grant me the courage to speak my truth with love and clarity, and the grace to listen with an open heart.

May my family find strength and peace in understanding my wishes. Amen.

Action Steps

- Schedule a time to talk with your family and trusted friends about your plan.
- Gather your documents and prepare to share their location and contents.
- Introduce your executor, trustee, or guardians and explain their roles.
- Encourage questions and patience with emotions.
- Follow up regularly to keep everyone informed and involved.

Part VI: Community, Grief, and Healing

You Don't Have to Carry This Alone

Chapter 25: Community, Support, and Spiritual Strength

"You don't have to carry this alone."

Preparing for the end of life is overwhelming.

The responsibility of securing your children's future, putting your affairs in order, and facing your own mortality can feel unbearably heavy.

But there's a powerful truth in this journey:

you are not meant to walk it alone.

There is strength in asking for help, and peace in knowing you are supported — emotionally, legally, and spiritually.

This chapter will guide you in building a circle of support that sustains you during this profound time.

Emotional Support: The Power of Connection

No one should navigate this path alone. Whether you have close family, trusted friends, or a community, these connections are your anchor, even when it feels like your world is shrinking.

Lean on those who love you.

- Share your fears, hopes, and needs. Opening up is a form of release and allows others to support you in meaningful ways.

Build a support network of trusted individuals.

- Include people with specific skills or experiences—friends who've faced similar journeys, or those with legal knowledge who can guide important decisions.

Find a therapist or counselor.

- Professional support helps manage anxiety, grief, and complex emotions. Your mental well-being is just as vital as your physical health.

Legal Support: Preparing for the Future

Legal planning ensures your children are cared for according to your wishes.

Create a will and designate guardianship.

- Without a will, the state decides who raises your children and manages your estate. Work with an estate planning attorney and choose a guardian who understands the responsibility.

Set up financial protection.

- Work with a financial planner to secure funds for your children's education, living expenses, and future needs through life insurance, trusts, or savings accounts.

Organize important documents.

- Keep wills, powers of attorney, insurance policies, healthcare directives, and financial accounts in one accessible place, and share with trusted individuals.

Spiritual Support: Anchoring in Faith and Hope

Spirituality, whatever form it takes, can be a source of comfort and clarity.

Seek spiritual counsel.

- Reach out to faith leaders for support, prayers, and rituals that bring peace to you and your family.

Create personal rituals and reflections.

- Journal, pray, meditate, or simply sit in silence to reflect on your life, legacy, and hopes.

Embrace community rituals.

- Gather with others through church, support groups, or friends who understand your journey. Shared presence brings healing and solidarity.

Finding Hope in Your Legacy

The deepest peace comes from knowing your love will endure. By surrounding yourself with support, securing your children's future, and nurturing your spiritual peace, you create a legacy of love that will guide your children through life's joys and struggles.

Though preparing for death feels daunting, it's also a beautiful opportunity to shape a future filled with hope and strength — a future where your values live on and your children are held in love.

Reflection | Prayer | Affirmation | Action

Community, Support, and Spiritual Strength — You Don't Have to Carry This Alone

Reflection Questions

1. Who in my life can I lean on for emotional, legal, and spiritual support?
2. How comfortable am I with asking for help and accepting it?
3. What spiritual practices bring me peace and strength?
4. How can I build a support system that sustains me and my children?

Affirmation

I am not alone. I am surrounded by love, support, and strength. Together, we carry this journey with grace and courage.

Prayer

God, Help me find comfort in the presence of others and peace in Your guidance.

Surround me with a loving community, steady my heart, and nurture my spirit through this journey.

May I feel supported, seen, and held every step of the way. Amen.

Action Steps

- Identify loved ones and trusted individuals to build your support network.
- Reach out to a therapist or counselor if needed.
- Meet with an estate planning attorney to finalize your will and guardianship.
- Work with a financial planner to secure your children's future.
- Organize all important documents in one accessible place.
- Connect with your spiritual community or create personal rituals for comfort.
- Share your journey with trusted friends or groups for mutual support.

Chapter 26: Memory, Celebration, and Ritual

The stories you leave behind can guide your children long after you are gone.

While planning for the end of life is often practical, it can also be deeply beautiful. Creating ways to celebrate your life, share your memories, and leave personal messages for your children allows your love to continue speaking when you no longer can.

This chapter offers ideas for legacy projects, pre-planned celebrations, and meaningful rituals that honor your story.

Legacy Projects

Legacy projects are simple, tangible ways to preserve your memories and wisdom.

Consider:

- Memory books or journals: Fill them with stories about your life, family traditions, and your hopes for your children.
- Video messages: Record short videos sharing your love, advice, or memories.
- Recipe collections: Pass down favorite meals and the stories behind them.

You don't have to finish everything perfectly. Even small pieces of your story will mean the world to your children.

Pre-Planned Celebrations

Some families find peace in planning a celebration of life in advance. This can be as simple or elaborate as you wish.

- Choose music or readings that reflect your spirit.
- Write down your wishes for how you'd like to be remembered.
- Consider creating a time capsule to be opened on a special date.

Pre-planning removes uncertainty and allows your family to focus on honoring your life.

Writing Letters to Open Later

One of the most profound gifts you can leave is your words.

Write letters your children can open on important milestones:

- Birthdays
- Graduations
- Weddings
- Moments when they need encouragement or reassurance

These letters will become treasures—reminders that your love endures.

🕊 Reflection | Prayer | Affirmation | Action

Memory, Celebration, and Ritual

Reflection Questions

1. What stories or wisdom do I most want to pass on to my children?
2. What would I want my celebration of life to feel like?
3. What milestones might my children face that I want to speak into?

Affirmation

My love will outlast my lifetime. My words and memories will be a guiding light for my children.

Prayer

God, Thank You for the gift of memory and the power of love that transcends time.

Help me create a legacy of joy, faith, and hope that will comfort my children all their lives. Amen.

Action Steps

- Start a memory journal or scrapbook this week.
- Record a short video message to your children.

- Write a letter for a future milestone (graduation, wedding, first job).
- Make a list of your wishes for your celebration of life.
- Gather any recipes, photos, or keepsakes you want to pass down.

Chapter 27: Losing a Parent or Loved One

"It doesn't feel okay. But it will be okay."

Losing a parent—or any loved one—is a moment that shakes your entire foundation. Even if you thought you were prepared, nothing truly softens the ache of that final goodbye.

This chapter is here to help you walk through the essential steps, so you don't have to carry the burden alone. Take each task one at a time, and remember: there is no rush.

You deserve space to grieve and heal while still honoring your loved one's legacy.

Things to do after losing a loved one

1. Notify Family and Friends

One of the first things you will need to do is let close family members and friends know about the passing. While this can feel overwhelming, it often becomes a moment of shared comfort.

As you make these calls, remember: you don't have to explain everything right away. Simply share the news and let them know you'll be in touch as arrangements come together.

Tip: Ask a trusted person to help you make calls or send messages so you don't have to do it alone.

2. Give Yourself Time to Grieve

You don't have to be strong every moment of the day. It's okay to feel the sadness, anger, confusion, or even relief that can come when someone you love passes away.

Allow yourself to:

- Take time off work or school if you need it.
- Decline invitations and rest.
- Cry without apologizing.
- Talk to someone you trust about your feelings.

If you need extra support, these organizations offer free grief help:

- Grief Anonymous
- VITAS Healthcare
- Grieving.com
- The Neptune Society's 12 Weeks of Peace online program

3. Choose a Funeral or Memorial Provider

When you feel ready, begin making arrangements. A funeral home, cremation provider, or place of worship can walk you through the process step by step.

A reputable provider will help with:

- Filing the death certificate
- Coordinating memorial or funeral services
- Providing copies of documents you'll need later

4. Gather Important Documents

You will need several copies of the death certificate—most families order at least 10. Keep originals in a secure place and treat copies with care, as they contain personal information.

Other documents to locate:

- Your loved one's will or trust
- Life insurance policies
- Property titles or deeds
- Vehicle titles
- Social Security card
- Veteran records (like the DD-214)

5. Notify Key Contacts and Agencies

Start with these steps:

- Call your loved one's doctor to request medical records if needed
- Notify Social Security Administration and any pension providers
- Contact life insurance companies to begin claims

- Let banks and credit card companies know of the passing

This process can feel endless, so take it one call at a time.

6. Secure Accounts and Property

To prevent identity theft and protect assets:

- Close or transfer bank accounts
- Cancel credit cards
- Stop automatic bill payments and subscriptions
- Lock up valuables and secure the home

If you find any safe deposit boxes, contact the bank to ask what documentation you'll need to access them.

7. Transfer Property and Vehicles

If you are the executor or administrator, you will need to begin transferring titles on homes, cars, or other property.

Usually, you'll need:

- A certified copy of the death certificate
- The will or trust documents
- Your identification

A probate or estate attorney can guide you if you are unsure.

8. Distribute Remaining Assets

If your loved one left a will or trust, follow the instructions to distribute property and funds. If there is no will, the estate will be settled according to state law.

It can help to keep detailed records of what you do, who you speak to, and where items go.

9. Care for Yourself

This is an emotionally exhausting time. Remember that you are allowed to:

- Take breaks from paperwork
- Say no to non-urgent demands
- Ask for help
- Seek professional grief counseling

This process can feel like too much when your heart is already hurting.

But step by step, you will get through it.

As you move forward, remember that your love for your parent or loved one doesn't end here. It lives on in your memories, your values, and the way you care for yourself and your family in their honor.

And remember:

"It doesn't feel okay. But it will be okay. God got You"

🕊 Reflection | Prayer | Affirmation | Action

Losing a Parent or Loved One

Reflection Questions

Take a few quiet moments to sit with these questions. You don't have to write anything down unless you want to—just let your thoughts come without judgment.

1. What are some of your favorite memories with your parent or loved one?
2. What part of this process feels the heaviest for you right now?
3. Who in your life can you lean on for comfort and help?
4. What do you want to remember about your loved one's spirit, humor, or wisdom?

Affirmation

Even in my sorrow, I am held in love. I have the strength to take each step, and I will allow myself to heal at my own pace.

Prayer

God, I come to You with a heart that feels broken and tired.

I ask for Your comfort to surround me as I grieve this loss.

Hold me steady when I feel overwhelmed, and remind me that I am not alone in this journey.

Help me honor my loved one's memory with grace and courage. Amen.

Action Steps

- Choose one or two actions you can take today to care for your heart and move forward gently.
- Reach out to a trusted friend or counselor to share how you're feeling.
- Light a candle or create a small space to honor your loved one's memory.
- Schedule time to rest without guilt.
- Make a simple list of the next practical steps you need to take, so they don't swirl around in your mind.

Checklist: After a Loved One Passes

Immediate Steps:
- Notify close family and friends
- Find a funeral or memorial provider
- Order at least 10 copies of the death certificate

Documents to Gather:
- Will or trust
- Insurance policies
- Property deeds
- Vehicle titles
- Social Security card
- Veteran records (DD-214)

Secure Assets:
- Lock up valuables
- Cancel credit cards
- Stop automatic bill payments
- Notify banks

Notify Agencies and Companies:
- Social Security Administration
- Life insurance companies
- Pensions or retirement funds

- Credit bureaus (to help prevent identity theft)

Property and Vehicles:
- Transfer titles with proper documents
- Close or transfer bank accounts

Care for Yourself:
- Take breaks
- Lean on friends and family
- Consider grief counseling
- Allow time to rest and heal

Worksheet: Notes and Next Steps

People I Need to Notify:

Important Documents to Locate:

Agencies/Companies to Call:

Funeral or Memorial Wishes:

_____

_____

How I Will Take Care of Myself:

Part VII: Your Legacy of Love

Purpose: Equip you with everything you need to put your plans in motion.

Chapter 28: Set Your Estate Planning Goals

Before you begin creating your estate plan, it's important to get clear on your goals.

Estate planning isn't just about having a will—it's about making thoughtful decisions that reflect your values, protect your loved ones, and ensure your wishes are honored.

Your goals will serve as the foundation for every decision you make throughout this process. Here are some common estate planning goals to consider:

24 Common Estate Planning Goals:
1. Pass on your assets efficiently
2. Ensure your money and property are transferred to your loved ones quickly and with minimal complications.
3. Provide financial security for your family
4. Make sure your loved ones are supported financially after you're gone.
5. Avoid probate court
6. Prevent your family from going through the long, stressful, and expensive probate process.
7. Protect your privacy

8. Keep your financial matters and asset transfers private and out of public court records.
9. Minimize taxes and legal fees
10. Preserve more of your wealth by reducing unnecessary costs during asset transfer.
11. Plan for medical emergencies or incapacity
12. Clearly document your wishes in case you become unable to make decisions for yourself.
13. Appoint trusted decision-makers
14. Choose people you trust to handle your affairs, distribute your assets, or make healthcare decisions on your behalf.
15. Support special circumstances
16. Protect the benefits of a loved one with special needs, or set boundaries for a beneficiary struggling with addiction.
17. Plan for minor children
18. Name guardians and create a financial plan to care for your children if you're no longer here.
19. Establish a business succession plan
20. If you own a business, decide how it will be managed or transferred after your passing.
21. Include charitable giving
22. Leave a legacy by directing assets to a charity or cause that matters to you.
23. Specify funeral or healthcare preferences
24. Make your wishes known for your end-of-life care and memorial arrangements.

Why These Goals Matter

Clarifying your estate planning goals now will guide the entire process. When you're facing emotional or complex decisions, referring back to your goals will help you stay aligned with your true intentions.

Whether your top priority is protecting your children, reducing taxes, or ensuring a peaceful transition for your family, your plan should reflect what matters most to you.

So take some time. Think about your priorities. Then use your goals to shape a plan that brings peace of mind—not just to you, but to those you love most.

🦬 Reflection | Prayer | Affirmation | Action

Set Your Estate Planning Goals

Reflection Questions

Pause here and ask yourself:

1. What do I most want my estate plan to accomplish?
2. Who am I trying to protect or provide for?
3. What values or lessons do I want to pass on through my planning?
4. What is one thing about this process that feels overwhelming—and who could I ask for help?

Affirmation

I am capable of making clear, loving choices. My planning today is a gift of peace for tomorrow.

Prayer

God, thank You for giving me the wisdom and courage to prepare for the future.

Help me make decisions that reflect my love and protect the people I care about most.

When I feel anxious or unsure, remind me that You are guiding me every step of the way. Amen.

Action Steps

Choose one or two next steps to start moving forward:

- Write down your top three estate planning priorities.
- Schedule a consultation with an estate planning attorney.
- Review your existing documents and note what needs updating.
- Talk with your family about your wishes and why they matter to you.

Estate Planning Goals Worksheet

Use this space to clarify your personal priorities and create a plan that truly reflects your wishes.

Step 1: What Matters Most to You?

Check the boxes that apply, and feel free to add your own goals.

My priorities include:

- ○ Making sure my family is financially supported
- ○ Avoiding probate court and unnecessary legal fees
- ○ Keeping my financial matters private
- ○ Making medical decisions in advance in case of incapacity
- ○ Ensuring my children are cared for and supported
- ○ Leaving something behind for a charity or cause I care about
- ○ Protecting a loved one with special needs
- ○ Managing how assets are passed down to someone with addiction or financial issues
- ○ Outlining my preferences for healthcare and funeral arrangements
- ○ Creating a succession plan for my business
- ○ Naming someone I trust to handle my estate
- ○ Minimizing taxes and maximizing the value of what I leave behind
- ○ Other: _____

Step 2: In Your Own Words

Take a few minutes to write down what you want your estate plan to accomplish.

What do you want to protect or prioritize through your estate plan?

Who do you want to provide for?

Are there specific things you want to give, and to whom?

Do you have any concerns (e.g., special needs, addiction, conflict)?

Do you want to support a cause or organization with part of your estate?

Do you have specific healthcare or end-of-life preferences?

Step 3: Your Next Steps

Based on your goals, here are a few actions you might consider:

- Meet with an estate planning attorney
- Create or update your will
- Set up a living trust
- Designate a medical power of attorney
- Complete an advance directive
- Purchase or review life insurance
- Set up a plan for minor children or dependents
- Organize financial and legal documents in one place
- Communicate your wishes with your loved ones

Keep this worksheet with your records, and revisit it each year or after any major life changes.

🦬 Reflection | Prayer | Affirmation | Action
Estate Planning Goals Worksheet

Reflection

Before you begin filling out forms or choosing legal documents, take a moment to center yourself.

1. What legacy do you want to leave—not just financially, but emotionally and spiritually?
2. What fears rise up when you think about planning your estate?

Acknowledge those fears, but don't let them rule you. Instead, let your love for your family lead the way.

Ask yourself:

1. What values do I want my estate plan to reflect?
2. Who are the people I most want to protect?
3. What unfinished emotional business should I resolve now, while I still can?

Affirmation

"My planning today brings peace tomorrow."

Prayer for Clarity and Courage

God, as I prepare for what I hope is a long way off, grant me the strength to face these decisions with clarity.

Remove the fear that clouds my thinking, and replace it with wisdom and love.

Help me be intentional—not just about documents and money, but about the legacy of faith, compassion, and protection I leave behind. Let my planning become an act of love, not fear. Amen.

Action Steps

- Complete the Estate Planning Goals Worksheet
- Use the prompts provided in this chapter to clarify what matters most to you.
- Prioritize your top 3 goals
- Circle or highlight the three most urgent or emotionally significant goals you want to tackle first.
- Schedule a consultation with an estate planning attorney
- If possible, begin forming your planning team now—this may include an attorney, financial advisor, and a trusted family member.
- Commit to one goal this week

Whether it's listing your assets or writing down your funeral preferences, take one tangible step toward peace.

Chapter 29: Your Legacy of Love

"When you leave this world, all that remains is the love you gave."

You have traveled through some of the most tender, courageous, and vulnerable parts of yourself to prepare for what most people spend a lifetime avoiding.

You have faced your fears so your children and loved ones will never have to wonder what you wanted.

You have made hard decisions with love as your compass.

This is your legacy.

- It is not just a collection of papers or legal forms—it is a living, breathing gift of peace.
- It is the comfort of knowing your children will be protected.
- It is the reassurance that your voice and values will carry on.
- It is the quiet, unshakable strength of a mother whose love reaches beyond her lifetime.

Take a moment to acknowledge all you have done.

You are not merely planning for death—you are affirming life.

You are planting seeds of security and faith that will grow long after you are gone.

As you close this book, remember these two things:

1. You have already given your family the greatest gift.
2. You have loved them enough to prepare.

A Letter to My Readers

Dear Mama, If you've made it to the final pages, please pause and give yourself credit. You have faced what most people spend a lifetime trying to avoid.

You have planned, prepared, and created a legacy of love. It doesn't matter if your plans are perfect. What matters is that you showed up with your whole heart for the people you love most.

My hope is that this book has made you feel less alone—that it has given you tools, comfort, and a sense of control in a season that can feel anything but.

I hope you will return to these pages whenever you feel uncertain or afraid. I hope you will share this guide with another mom who needs to know she is not alone.

And above all, I hope you will remember that this is not the end—It is the beginning of a legacy defined by courage, compassion, and unwavering love.

You are prepared. You are enough. You are never alone.

Keep going. Keep believing. You are doing the bravest work there is.

With all my respect and love, Shaun the Mom

Final Prayer

Heavenly Father,

Thank You for guiding us through the uncertainties of life. I pray for courage, clarity, and peace for every mother reading these words. May she feel Your presence as she makes decisions for her family's future.

Bless her hands that plan, her heart that loves, and her mind that organizes. May her legacy be one of hope, faith, and unwavering love. Surround her with support, comfort, and wisdom as she navigates difficult choices.

Let her know, Lord, that she is never alone, and that every act of preparation is a reflection of her love. Protect her family, honor her efforts, and guide her always in Your light.

Amen.

Scriptures for Peace & Eternal Hope

John 14:27 (NLT)

Peace I leave with you; my peace I give you. I do not give to you as the world gives.

Philippians 4:7 (NLT)

The peace of God, which surpasses all understanding, will guard your hearts and minds in Christ Jesus.

Psalm 23:1-3 (NLT)

The Lord is my shepherd; I have all that I need. He lets me rest in green meadows; He leads me beside peaceful streams.

Revelation 21:4 (NLT)

He will wipe every tear from their eyes. There will be no more death or mourning or crying or pain.

Closing Prayer:

Lord, fill my heart with Your perfect peace. Help me trust in Your eternal promises and rest fully in Your love.

Book Club / Group Discussion Questions

1. What part of Shaundra's story felt most familiar or inspiring to you?
2. What fears or thoughts came up for you while reading about end-of-life planning?
3. How do you currently talk (or avoid talking) with your children or loved ones about your health?
4. What does "peaceful planning" mean to you personally?
5. Which chapter helped you feel more empowered to make legal or financial decisions?
6. How has your view of legacy changed after reading this book?
7. What are the biggest emotional blocks you face when it comes to planning for the future?
8. How do you define "love after diagnosis" in your own life?
9. What support do you wish existed for moms with chronic illness in your community?
10. How does your faith or spirituality show up in your planning or caregiving?
11. What one action step from the book are you committed to doing in the next 30 days?
12. Who would you recommend this book to—and why?

Glossary of Key Terms

A–C

Advance Directive: A legal document outlining your wishes for medical care if you can't communicate them.

Annuity: A financial product providing regular payments over time, often used for retirement or long-term planning.

Beneficiary: A person or entity designated to receive assets from a will, trust, or insurance policy.

Beneficiary Designation: Instructions for who will receive certain accounts (e.g., life insurance, retirement funds) separate from a will.

Charitable Bequest: A gift left to a charity through your will or trust.

Community Property: Property acquired during marriage that is legally considered jointly owned in certain states.

D–F

Digital Assets: Online accounts, social media profiles, cryptocurrencies, and other online property.

Digital Estate Plan: Instructions for managing online accounts, passwords, and digital content after death.

Do Not Resuscitate (DNR): Instructions specifying not to perform CPR or life-saving measures.

Durable Power of Attorney: Legal authority to make financial or legal decisions if you become incapacitated.

Executor / Personal Representative: The person responsible for carrying out the instructions in a will.

Ethical Will / Legacy Letter: A letter or document sharing your values, life lessons, and personal messages to loved ones.

Estate Planning: Organizing your assets, finances, and wishes to ensure they are managed and distributed according to your intentions.

Estate Inventory: A detailed list of all assets, debts, and property for legal and planning purposes.

Estate Tax: Taxes that may be owed on assets transferred after death.

Family Bank / Education Fund: Financial arrangements to support children's education or family needs.

Family Meeting / Estate Meeting: A gathering to discuss your estate, legacy, and final wishes with loved ones.

Funeral / Burial Plan: A document specifying your wishes for funeral, burial, or cremation services.

Funeral Preplanning: Documenting your funeral wishes and possibly paying for services ahead of time.

G–I

Guardianship: A legal arrangement where someone is appointed to care for a minor child or dependent adult.

Guardianship Nomination: A written statement naming your preferred guardian for minor children in your will.

HIPAA Authorization: A form allowing healthcare providers to share your medical information with designated individuals.

Inheritance Tax: Taxes imposed by some states on assets received by beneficiaries.

Intestate: Dying without a valid will; state laws determine asset distribution.

J–L

Joint Accounts: Bank or investment accounts shared by two or more people.

Joint Tenancy / Right of Survivorship: Property ownership where assets automatically pass to co-owners upon death.

Legacy Project: A creative way to leave memories, guidance, or family history for future generations.

Letter of Instruction: An informal note providing guidance to family or executors beyond the legal documents (like account logins or personal wishes).

Life Insurance: A policy that pays a lump sum to beneficiaries after death.

Life Story / Memoir: Recording your personal history and lessons to leave a lasting legacy.

Living Trust: A trust created during your lifetime to hold assets, often avoiding probate.

Living Will: Specifies what medical treatments you want or don't want if you are terminally ill or permanently unconscious.

Ladybird Deed: A type of property deed used in some states to transfer real estate while retaining control during your lifetime.

M–P

Medical Power of Attorney: Someone authorized to make healthcare decisions if you cannot.

Minor Trust: A trust set up to hold assets for a child until they reach a specified age.

Mortgage: A loan used to purchase real estate; may affect estate planning decisions.

Payable-on-Death (POD) / Transfer-on-Death (TOD): Designations that allow certain accounts or assets to transfer directly to a named beneficiary without probate.

Personal Property Memorandum: A list specifying who should receive personal items (jewelry, furniture, keepsakes).

Palliative Care: Medical care focused on comfort and quality of life for people with serious illnesses.

Probate: The legal process of validating a will and distributing assets under court supervision.

R–S

Prepaid Funeral Contract: A plan arranged ahead of time to cover funeral costs, protecting loved ones from financial burden.

Retirement Accounts (401k, IRA): Accounts designed to save for retirement, often with beneficiary designations.

Revocable Trust: A type of living trust you can change or revoke during your lifetime.

Special Needs Trust: A trust created to provide for a person with disabilities without affecting eligibility for government benefits.

Succession Plan: A plan for transferring management of a business or assets after death or incapacity.

T–Z

Trust Fund: Money or property held in a trust for the benefit of a person or organization.

Trustee: The person or institution that manages a trust according to its terms.

Veterans Benefits: Government benefits available to veterans, which may include survivor benefits or burial assistance.

Resources and Support

Estate Planning and Legal Support

- Nolo – www.nolo.com – Affordable legal guides and templates
- Trust & Will – www.trustandwill.com – Simple online estate planning
- Local Legal Aid Societies – Free or low-cost help for qualifying families

Grief and Emotional Support

- Grief Anonymous – www.griefanonymous.com
- The Dougy Center – www.dougy.org – Support for grieving children and families
- VITAS Healthcare Bereavement Resources – www.vitas.com/family-and-caregiver-support/grief-and-bereavement

Parenting and Single Motherhood

- National Crittenton – www.nationalcrittenton.org

- Single Mothers by Choice – www.singlemothersbychoice.org

Planning Tools and Templates

- Everplans – www.everplans.com – Digital vault for storing documents and wishes
- Cake – www.joincake.com – End-of-life planning tools
- CaringInfo.org – Advance Directive forms
- AARP End-of-Life Planning Resources – www.aarp.org

The Warrior Mom's Guide™ Book Series

FOUNDATION: The Pilot Book

♡ A Warrior Within, A Chronic Illness

The Warrior Mom's Guide to Sickle Cell & Chronic Resilience

My story of battling sickle cell while raising a family—woven with practical mindset shifts, survival tools, and advocacy.

📖 The heart of the Warrior Mom movement and the introduction to the series.

THE DEEP-DIVE SERIES (Books 1–10)

♡ **The Warrior Mom's Guide to GhettoOCD™**
(Home Organization & Cleaning)

Practical, real-life homemaking strategies for moms with chronic illness.

❀ The Warrior Mom's Guide to Mental Wellness & Finding Joy in the Chaos

Therapy, prayer, and emotional survival tools for weary moms.

🤍 The Warrior Mom's Guide to Single Motherhood by Choice

Reclaiming peace, health, and wholeness after carrying it all.

🤍 The Warrior Mom's Guide to Loving Unexpectedly

Guardianship, Fostering & Adoption with Faith and Fierce Love

Finding your voice, courage, and confidence in nontraditional motherhood.

🤍 The Warrior Mom's Guide to Generational Wealth & Family Legacy

Building wealth, purpose, and a future that lasts.

🖤 The Warrior Mom's Guide to Spiritual Reset & Chronic Faith

Faith after diagnosis, grace during flare-ups, and spiritual renewal when you feel forgotten.

⬤ The Warrior Mom's Guide to ZBB & Cash Stuffing (Finances)

Zero-based budgeting & cash envelope systems for sick-day survival.

📚 The Warrior Mom's Guide to Homeschooling for the Homegirls

Practical tools for rest, rejuvenation, and chronic-illness-friendly homeschooling.

🖤 The Warrior Mom's Guide to Homeownership & Stability

Creative paths to securing a home with chronic illness and limited income.

🌿 The Warrior Mom's Guide to Living in Peace

End-of-life planning with grace: wills, medical directives, legacy projects, and restoration.

Find the books, companion workbooks, journals, planners, and more at:

www.warriormomacademy.com

About the Author

Shaundra Harris is a writer, mother, and advocate for families navigating chronic illness and life transitions. After her own journey of preparing for the unexpected, she became passionate about equipping other moms with practical tools, hope, and a sense of community.

Through her books, workshops, and online resources, Shaundra helps women face their fears and build legacies of love.

When she's not writing, you can find her spending time with her children, creating community, and reminding other women that they are stronger than they know.

Acknowledgments

This book was made possible by the love and encouragement of so many.

To my family—thank you for giving me the inspiration to keep going, even on the hardest days.

To my friends and mentors—your wisdom helped me find the words to share this message.

To every mother reading this—thank you for your bravery. You are my reason for writing.

Writing this book has been a journey of love, faith, and unflinching honesty. It would not exist without the people who held me up while I learned to let go.

To my children: You are the reason I wake up and the reason I keep going. Every plan I make and every word I write is for you.

To the mothers in my community who shared their stories with courage—I honor you.

To every reader: Thank you for trusting me to walk with you through some of the hardest questions we face. May you find peace, hope, and strength here.

www.ingramcontent.com/pod-product-compliance
Lightning Source LLC
Chambersburg PA
CBHW021156160426
43194CB00007B/758